Shingijutsu

The Art of Discovery and Learning

∞,

改善

∞,

Ralph Wood
Michael Herscher
Bob Emiliani

Shingijutsu-Kaizen: The Art of Discovery and Learning / Ralph Wood, Michael Herscher, and Bob Emiliani.

Cover illustration by N.C.
Cover design by Bob Emiliani and Katsusaburo Yoshino
Illustrations by Mary Crombie Geer, www.acornstudio.biz

ISBN-13: 978-0-9898631-5-5

Library of Congress Control Number: 2015948213

1. Organizational Improvement 2. Kaizen 3. Leadership
4. Business 5. Economics 6. Lean

First Edition: October 2015

Published by The Center for Lean Business Management, LLC, Wethersfield, Conn., USA

This publication provides accurate information with respect to the subject matter covered. It is sold with the understanding that it does not in any way represent legal, financial, business, consulting, or other professional service.

Manufactured using digital print-on-demand technology.

Together we create a harmonious future.

CONTENTS

PREFACE

Shingijutsu USA Corporation consultants have been helping organizations improve processes by teaching people methods and tools rooted in flow production. But, they do much more than that. Perhaps the most important thing one learns is how to think. Kaizen is the means for doing this. You learn, as never before, how to understand abnormal conditions and how to quickly correct abnormalities by both trial-and-error and experiments.

Shingijutsu-Kaizen is the most powerful way to grow as a person while simultaneously improving both business and humanity. The way in which Shingijutsu teaches and how people learn has always been personal, handed from the sensei (teacher) to student one-by-one and in small groups. While this method has been very effective, it obviously has limited reach. The challenges that business and society face in the future demand that a wider audience learn Kaizen and its beneficial role in developing people and organizations.

It is important to correctly learn the technical aspects of Kaizen, which are rooted in industrial engineering practices. Many people think they know these basics, but they do not. Knowledge without practice is pretend knowledge. Knowledge must be fact-based, and facts can only be discerned through direct, hands-on engagement. This includes management as well as workers.

More than that, however, there must also be excitement for Kaizen. The spirit of new ideas and discovery, the thrill of creativity and innovation, the challenge of simplicity, and a tireless quest for new knowledge must exist. Management serves a critically important role in generating excitement for Kaizen. It begins with the CEO and includes all levels of management in every functional area. It is our aim to convey elements of the technical aspects of Kaizen and especially human excitement for Kaizen by giving concrete examples.

Leadership commitment and enthusiasm for Kaizen are often missing from organizations. This is a grave error. While there are many secrets to successful flow production, Kaizen is foremost among them. An organization cannot be "Lean" without doing Kaizen – a lot of Kaizen.

Kaizen is fundamental and must be practiced by everyone, every day. It is the human resource development practice. It creates a culture that asks "Why?" It promotes ideas, creativity, and innovation. Kaizen, itself, is the change management practice. It fosters teamwork and relationship-building. It helps you see reality. It is how you identify future leaders. It is how to simultaneously improve quality, costs, lead-time, safety, and so on. There is far more to Kaizen than meets the eye.

Nearly everyone wants to improve their capabilities, their processes, and their work relationships. Kaizen offers the opportunity to do that and more. It is our hope that readers will gain much from this book and return to it again and again to deepen their understanding of Kaizen and of human potential.

This book is a humble attempt to share our understanding of the spirit, mindset, and methods of Shingijutsu USA and their approach to improving the human condition. It is derived from our participation in Kaizen, our observation of Kaizen, and our study of Kaizen. Please recognize that a book can only present an approximation of Shingijutsu's methods for teaching people Kaizen. And, both their methods and what we have learned from them will certainly grow and improve over time, while the contents of a book remain static.

If you get one message from this book, we hope you realize how unique and sincere Shingijutsu sensei are as they have worked to rid the world of waste while simultaneously developing human potential. We hope you are likewise motivated to engage in this virtuous effort.

Ralph Wood
Glastonbury, Connecticut

Michael Herscher
Renton, Washington

Bob Emiliani
Wethersfield, Connecticut

ACKNOWLEDGMENTS

The authors wish to sincerely thank the following organizations and people:

Mary Crombie Geer of Acorn Studio, Glastonbury, Connecticut, for drawing the scenes with human characters to illustrate various points in the text.

The hospital, the aircraft engine repair center, and the office furniture manufacturer whose genba Kaizen lessons appear in Chapters 5, 6, and 7.

The skillful and dedicated work of Shingijutsu Kaizen consultants, upon which Part III, Genba Kaizen Lessons, is based.

Rudy Go, Katsusaburo Yoshino, Hirohiko Eto, and the leaders of Shingijutsu USA Corporation.

どうもありがとうございました。

Disclosure:

INTRODUCTION

A vision propagated by technically skilled and persuasive persons is a powerful instrument for transformation. This book tells the story of a company, Shingijutsu USA Corporation, and the people who joined together to realize a particular vision: to help others around the world understand and create their own methods of flow production.

In the face of all that has been written about Kaizen, what can you, perhaps a business leader, a functional leader, a plant manager, or an operator, learn from this book? First, through the voices of both Shingijutsu's customers and senior sensei (teachers), you will learn about Shingijutsu's time-tested philosophy and methods for rapidly improving processes and developing people.

You will also learn how Shingijutsu has applied their methods to many different kinds of businesses – original equipment manufacturers, retailers, maintenance and repair facilities, engineering organizations, construction contractors, banks, technology businesses, and hospitals – in many different countries of the world.

You will learn the profound lessons that others have learned by working directly with Shingijutsu. You will come to understand how they evolved from their founding in 1987 and learned from its experiences with different cultures and clients. You will learn how Shingijutsu assesses an organization against the processes and indicators that lead to results. You will also learn that some of the methods have been misunderstood or misapplied by others and how to correct them.

This book is an important work because it illuminates a critically important feature of how to create flow production that many people are unaware of or do not understand. This book makes several valuable new contributions:

- Fills a void in our understanding of the history and expansion of flow production outside of the auto industry, post-1987.
- Recognizes Shingijutsu's pioneering role in helping people discover and learn the things necessary to practice flow production.

- Introduces Shingijutsu USA to people who have only heard of them second- or third-hand, or who do not know Shingijutsu at all.
- Clarifies the "tough love" approach used by Shingijutsu Kaizen consultants, and illustrates its effectiveness in helping people learn and develop Kaizen spirit.
- Shows that Shingijutsu-Kaizen is fun and engaging, which, in turn, results in widespread participation and rapid improvement.
- Shares the unique thinking and actions to create material and information flow.
- Helps people recognize that their understanding of Kaizen is likely to be substantially different and, therefore, less impactful in practice than Shingijutsu-Kaizen.

This book is organized into four parts. The first part, Chapters 1 and 2, illuminates Shingijutsu's culture: its philosophy, values, deeply-held beliefs; its artifacts; and its language. The second part, Chapters 3 and 4, examines Shingijutsu's distinctive competencies.

The third part, Chapters 5, 6, and 7, presents lessons in how Shingijutsu's work plays out in practice. In these chapters, we present three case studies of Shingijutsu Kaizen with actual clients. The fourth part, Chapter 8, discusses "the basics," and adds Shingijutsu's philosophical perspectives to some of the important productivity methods and tools and seeks to redress some misconceptions about them. Chapter 9 addresses future challenges for business and society.

This book does not mention the names of Shingijutsu USA consultants or clients. Its purpose is not to aggrandize the company, but simply to inform interested persons on methods of improving processes and developing people that have proven to be very successful over time.

We remind readers that this book reflects our understanding of the spirit and methods of Kaizen taught by Shingijutsu USA, derived from our participation, observation, and study of Kaizen. Though it is an approximation of their methods, it nevertheless offers tremendous insights and knowledge that readers can use. We hope you will one day have the opportunity to personally experience Shingijutsu-Kaizen.

PART I

CULTURE

Convert the culture from complex to simple.

CHAPTER 1

PHILOSOPHY, VALUES, AND DEEPLY-HELD BELIEFS

Philosophy

Explaining the Japanese word "shingijutsu" reveals an essential foundation of Shingijutsu's philosophy. "Shin" in English means "new." "Gijutsu" means "technology;" but the root "jutsu" has the connotation of art, technique or competence that is gained through practice. Jutsu requires action. Learning to play golf requires constant practice even though the sport can be understood by anyone. Similarly, talking about "new technology" differs greatly from its actual practice.

In this light, when one interprets technology as accumulated knowledge that has been crafted into tools and artifacts for facilitating the accomplishment of human purposes, and when the purpose is production, the implications of the word "shingijutsu" become clearer: clients gain competence in a new (to them) production technology through rigorous practice, which is guided and reinforced by Shingijutsu's sensei. What emerges is production (and non-production) work that resembles an art form.

Another underpinning of Shingijutsu's philosophy comes from the concept and practice of Zen. Zen is often interpreted as "ideal state." The monks in Zen temples live disciplined lifestyles in pursuit of the ideal that is attributed to Buddha: art without form. Archery is sometimes practiced in Zen temples because ideal proficiency requires the disciplined union of deep mental control with physical prowess. Kaizen must be practiced in a similarly disciplined way.

Kaizen – often interpreted as "continuous improvement" – has a sacred place in Shingijutsu's philosophy, where it takes on the meaning "relentless improvement toward the ideal state." To be effective Kaizen must be a life-long journey; whence, Shingijutsu's motto "Kaizen Forever!" And, just as the Zen monks do with acolytes, Shingijutsu sensei apply "tough love" in their quest to help clients learn and improve. Tough love may involve light physical contact, or the waiving of arms or pulling of sleeves to suggest mock contact. More usually, however, tough love is delivered by oral scoldings.

A corollary to the philosophical elements of "learning through practice and relentless improvement" is Shingijutsu's policy of "do not teach," which is infused into all aspiring sensei. What a paradox: teachers who are not supposed to teach! Resolution is found in the concept of action learning, sometimes called discovery learning. Shingijutsu's sensei do not answer questions directly; instead, often citing an analogy that illustrates a relevant principle, they will turn the question back to the student in a way that promotes deeper thought and further action by the student. This reversal – a martial arts practice – is usually concluded with the instruction: "I want you to…." Meaning, learn how to do this through daily practice.

After discovering new knowledge, the student is expected to describe his or her new learning to the sensei, who is trained to give a binary response: "Okay" or "Failed." Now enters tough love: the "okay" response is often not accompanied by praise; the "failed" response, however, is customarily accompanied by scolding and a lesson or analogy intended to bring forth correction after more introspection and action on the part of the student. Sometimes, when a student has badly missed the point, or is not taking the learning experience or the sensei's instructions seriously, "failed" is replaced with "you're fired!"

The closest response to praise that a student will hear is a "left-handed" compliment, for example, "You are good, but not that good." This approach seems hard on the student, who, by the way, could even be the CEO of the client company; but for most people the elation that stems from their new learning and insights outweighs any temporary loss of pride. The other mitigating factor is the tremendous progress and many results that a client team will accomplish in just one week during a genba Kaizen under Shingijutsu's tutelage.

Senior Shingijutsu sensei are unlike other consultants, who are prescriptive, in that they deliver significant results by working at the genba – the physical location where work takes place and its surrounding environment and situation. Shingijutsu consultants guide people towards discovery so that the learning is far more substantive and meaningful.

One senior sensei, in particular, was criticized by an outside colleague who called him an "insultant." The colleague elaborated, "You insult your clients by acting like a big elephant in a pottery shop, breaking things." To which the sensei replied, "I am not breaking things that the client can sell; I am breaking only things that the client cannot sell."

The last key element of Shingijutsu's philosophy that we want to mention here is healthy skepticism. This philosophy is born of many experiences in which people manipulated facts and information, or presented misleading data and specious theories – sometimes unintentionally, sometimes intentionally. There is an old adage that when people are faced with a difficult goal, three kinds of behavior emerge:

- Some will distort the data
- Some will try very hard to realize the goal
- Some will distort the system

One Shingijutsu sensei states flatly, "Charts lie and people lie." What is Shingijutsu's antidote? It is the philosophy of "go see for yourself," which can be paraphrased as "mistrust and verify." Go where? To the genba, meaning the place where the actual work is performed.

Realization of the "genba philosophy" involves the following instructions. While making first-hand observations at the genba, be sure to use all five senses to detect abnormal conditions and waste. Remember that the senses involve seeing, listening, smelling, tasting and touching, but not talking. Make sketches of what you observe. Now ask yourself "Why?" multiple times to uncover the reasons that work occurs as it does, the root causes for any abnormalities and waste that you observed, and justifications for the data that you gathered. Deal with only objective (observable, measurable, reliable, specific) facts, not with theories, abstract concepts or subjective opinions. After these tasks are completed, discuss your findings with the client or with your team (including the sensei), and, jointly, formulate improvement challenges.

Values

The preceding elements of Shingijutsu's philosophy help motivate an understanding of the company's values or principles, of which we have identified four:

- Commitment to Kaizen comes first
- Learning comes from observation and practice: genba Kaizen
- Improvement and innovation come from people who learn and grow
- The future comes from innovation

The principle "commitment to Kaizen comes first" belongs to leadership. Shingijutsu views that it is leadership's role to create a management system for enabling Kaizen throughout the organization. Enabling Kaizen requires the alignment of improvement opportunities with corporate strategy and goals; the active and visible engagement of the leader; the establishment of a Kaizen Promotion Office (KPO) to help build an organizational intellect and capability for Kaizen, including sensei to train Kaizen team leaders and to help Kaizen teams; the alignment of policies and evaluation, reward and recognition systems with Kaizen; and the empowerment of everyone to become involved in Kaizen activities.

The committed leader must also have undergone training in Shingijutsu's methods and is expected to participate in Kaizen and support Kaizen teams. In some cases, leaders may also be qualified to deliver Kaizen training to associates. When an organization's leadership lacks this commitment, Shingijutsu may use draconian methods to gain commitment. One such method includes "firing" a key person by having him or her removed from a team or study mission and sending him or her away to think about the consequences of his or her actions.

The principle of "learning comes from observation and practice" is as old as recorded history; it is the basis of training in martial arts. Shingijutsu's success in "making people" rests on three foundations:

- Guiding people on "study missions," where they can observe flow production systems in action, learn new tools and practice them in a real genba;
- Putting people to work on Kaizen teams, after only brief classroom training;
- Providing feedback and correction meant to promote reflection and further self-discovery.

Figure 1-1 Sensei observing a team member and providing feedback.

With this approach, participants tend to retain 80 percent of what they learn as a result of "doing." In addition to skills gained through direct experience (practice), the brain also processes observation and indirect experience to encode learning and build performance capacity. Shingijutsu's discovery-learning approach, besides being very effective, has neuro-scientific validity.

The next principle, "improvement and innovation come from people who learn and grow," is often paraphrased by Shingijutsu sensei as "making people." This principle is born of the culture that people are the source of, and means for, quality, productivity and improvement. The sensei's main job, therefore, is to cultivate human talent for tasks such as problem-solving, quality and productivity improvement, creating new ideas and concepts, and testing new ideas and concepts. Particular skills involve system thinking, policy deployment, leading Kaizen teams, trystorming, using examples in nature, prototyping with existing resources (called "moonshine"), root causes analysis, mistake-proofing, 5S, standard work, and set-up reduction, to name several skills.

Earlier we touched on Shingijutsu's action learning process for developing people, and we will have more to say about this in Chapter 4. The principle of "making people" also embraces three personal responsibilities that everyone in the client's organization, as well as at Shingijutsu, is expected to undertake: responsibility for developing yourself; responsibility for developing the people beneath you; and responsibility for developing the people above you. When these interlocking responsibilities are carried out in earnest, organizational improvement follows quickly.

Shingijutsu's fourth principle, "the future comes from innovation," is built into every Kaizen engagement. Client teams are coached and encouraged to use their own wisdom and ingenuity, as opposed to money, to invent and create innovative solutions. The instruction "seek million-dollar ideas, not million-dollar machines" sums up the objective. Shingijutsu may launch a Kaizen team with a list of world-class characteristics as its improvement targets. These characteristics have derived from Shingijutsu's many engagements with companies world-wide.

Dependent on context, the list of characteristics held up to a Kaizen team may cover world-class design, world-class production or world-class logistics. Teams are shown how to develop new concepts by appealing to nature, and they are introduced to "moonshining," a practice whose name was borrowed from the covert distilling of alcohol, with the aid of apparatus resourcefully assembled from junk parts, in the back woods of the Appalachian mountains in the United States.

Kaizen teams also learn to develop and then winnow seven solution concepts for each abnormality; the final two or three concepts are then tested through simulation. In order for a Kaizen team's innovation to pass Shingijutsu's "muster," it must integrate people, material, information and equipment. Some Shingijutsu sensei, when particularly impressed by an innovation, may bestow a certificate to the originating team.

Deeply-Held Beliefs

People in an organization harbor shared, deeply-held beliefs and assumptions about the environment of the organization, about how the organization has succeeded in this environment, and about how they have succeeded within the organization. These tacit beliefs are deeply rooted in the history of the organization. They have evolved over time through a joint learning process of selection: those things that did not work were abandoned in favor of those things that did work. Through the subconscious conditioning of people's daily behavior, the shared, tacit beliefs bring stability and reassurance to the culture.

Shingijutsu sensei hold fast to a deeply-rooted belief about genba Kaizen and the need to continually improve toward "ideal" production by growing people and evolving knowledge. The assumption is that if an organization is performing Kaizen under Shingijutsu's coaching, the organization is learning and evolving.

At a more fundamental level is the belief that an organization's success resides in its operational capability, in the quality and in the productivity of what it does. Accompanying this belief is the assumption that Shingijutsu's methods can improve any organization or institution. The three case studies covered in Part III give credence to this assumption: one is a hospital, one is a maintenance and repair operation, and one is an original-equipment manufacturer.

There is also in Shingijutsu's culture a tacit assumption that the master-apprentice learning approach, which features a combination of observation, practice, reflection and correction, is the best way to educate, train and develop people, who will, in turn, become superior leaders of their organizations' evolution and even be able to teach Shingijutsu new lessons. There is a strong belief in the benefits of discipline and correction, sometimes scolding, in the learning process.

Behind the sometimes gruff exterior of a Shingijutsu sensei is a feeling of humility toward his client and the learning that both are experiencing. When something doesn't go well, or when a client is less than satisfied with an engagement, Shingijutsu's immediate response is that "it's our fault."

Finally, we highlight Shingijutsu's faith in standard work as a cornerstone of success. It is the most frequently cited element of the essential "basics" that Shingijutsu wants its clients to understand and practice. Standard work has three ingredients: production to customer demand; arrangement of all work into a sequence of activities; and maintenance of minimum levels of work in process. Another description of standard work is "Takt time, work sequence, and standard work in process." Standard work is a communication tool that tells everyone in the organization what is actually going on.

NOTES

What did you learn from this chapter?

What will you put into practice?

CHAPTER 2

ARTIFACTS AND LANGUAGE

Culture is comprised of things that you can observe: what you see, hear, smell, taste and feel as you travel around, observe, and experience the society or organization. It may include behaviors, policies, procedures, rights and status, totems, rituals, communications, decision-making, language and jargon, identity symbols, formality in authority relationships, and work-life balance, to name some. These are artifacts of a culture.

Illustration courtesy of N.C.

Figure 2-1. Shingijutsu cultural artifact depicting Moonshine.
It reads: "Continue moonshine to change to the ideal state."

After a little exposure to Shingijutsu, an observer soon discerns that sensei represent its culture and artifacts. They dress in black from head to toe, sometimes wearing tops that have embroidered, Kaizen-related kanji characters; they have been trained extensively to behave according to Shingijutsu's philosophy and values discussed in the previous chapter; and they command respect from their clients. The sensei are primarily older men who are slender in appearance and imbued with extraordinary stamina: they walk fast and may cover as many as six Kaizen teams several times a day during a week-long engagement of eight-hour days in a large facility. Some sensei may string together multiple engagements while on one trip away from home. Thus, the sensei's work-life balance is decidedly tipped toward work.

A behavior of Shingijutsu's sensei is that they will not hesitate to scold anyone – from executives to Kaizen team members to interpreters to apprentices. Scoldings are a ritual, and take place for an important purpose: to promote learning and improvement. Being on the receiving end of a scolding can be humiliating, and only the foolish would not heed the sensei's advice and risk another scolding. As disciples of Shingijutsu sensei, each of the authors has been told, "Your role is to observe and not to talk or to ask questions." "When the sensei speaks to you, you must acknowledge with 'hai' ('yes' in Japanese) and then discover on your own what he means." "You must never argue with the sensei." Your learning process of discovery involves asking yourself "Why?" multiple times until the sensei's true meaning or lesson becomes apparent to you. Then, as we said in the last chapter, you must return to the sensei and have your new learning validated.

Another aspect of Shingijutsu's culture is the interpreter, who is always at the shoulder of the sensei. Although many of Shingijutsu's sensei understand English, and often use English words and phrases when conversing, most feel more comfortable communicating with the help of an interpreter. The dynamic between sensei and the interpreter is interesting to watch. While the sensei respects the language skills of the interpreter, the sensei will not hesitate to tell interpreters that they have got either their Japanese or their English wrong, or to request correction of some irritating behavior.

One artifact is conspicuously missing from Shingijutsu's culture. This artifact is a library of documentation and teaching materials that usually accompanies a consulting company. Knowledge, therefore, flows directly from the sensei, who is quick to illustrate key concepts by drawing sketches and diagrams on flip charts, by explaining the origins of words, by relating to analogies, and, sometimes, by acting and miming.

Genba Kaizen is a ritual in Shingijutsu's culture. The ritual starts with a team showing the sensei what it proposes to do, followed by a tour of the genba. The sensei compares observations with the team and then commences to ask several "Why?" questions, which motivate the team's learning process. This first encounter of the team with the sensei concludes with the sensei issuing several challenges, which shape what the team does in the coming days.

At his second visit to the team's genba, the sensei usually knows whether or not the team is going to succeed in its goals for the Kaizen. Rather than continue a futile effort, the sensei may disband a poorly-functioning team at this point or ask one or more troublesome members to leave. Alternatively, the sensei may direct the team to re-study the "basics" before attempting to make further progress.

Shingijutsu has a body of knowledge and a learning and training model that is relatively transparent. Sensei are skilled in the practice of this model and are exceptionally well versed in the body of technical and interpersonal knowledge. And, Shingijutsu's sensei have assimilated many experiences in applying their model and body of knowledge to many different organizations and business endeavors besides production; they have evolved beyond production.

Shingijutsu manages knowledge and quality through the organizational position called "Jutsu Shu." This person is Shingijutsu's oracle, the owner and maintainer of its wisdom, knowledge, practices and art. Shingijutsu's sensei report to the Jutsu Shu their summaries of Kaizens with clients; in turn, the Jutsu Shu assimilates these results and may, if warranted, develop systemic adjustments to Shingijutsu's procedures. The Jutsu Shu then broadcasts the adjustments to all sensei, usually through the medium of periodic board meetings that are attended by all.

The authority structure in many organizations is topped in status by those people who control the money. Within Shingijutsu, authority is vested in who controls the knowledge, and this person is the Jutsu Shu.

By virtue of his superior command of Shingijutsu's knowledge and practice, he has attained the highest status in the organization. Sometimes, status is recognized by initials after a sensei's name; for example, one sensei's name carries the letters "F.O.M.," which stand for "Father of Moonshine."

One prevalent item of status in many companies is missing within Shingijutsu: The office at its headquarters in Japan is open, and the sensei have no desks or chairs. Everyone sits on the floor during board meetings. What is the reason for this office architecture? Quite simply, Shingijutsu's genba is the world, not its office.

A cherished possession of a team member who has gone through a genba Kaizen with Shingijutsu is the certificate of accomplishment signed by the sensei, shown in Figure 2-2. It is officially called a "License to Practice Kaizen Continuously." In some cases, the sensei will adorn this artifact with calligraphy in kanji characters that personalizes and conveys different messages.

SHINGIJUTSU USA CORPORATION

AWARDS THIS

LICENSE

TO

For Participation in the

KAIZEN WORKSHOP

Eastford, CT

July 28, 2014 – August 1, 2014

YOU ARE ALLOWED TO PRACTICE KAIZEN CONTINUOUSLY

次世代に
残す魂を
書こう。

Illustration by N.C.

Figure 2-2. Kaizen workshop certificate.

The language used by Shingijutsu sensei reflects unique features of the Japanese language as well as the development and evolution of flow production methods and of genba Kaizen. It is the language of never-ending questions, ideas, creativity, and improvement.

The Japanese language conveys meaning that helps one to understand the mindset and methods of Shingijutsu sensei so they can carry the tradition forward. Understanding and adopting this language will benefit you both intellectually and in your practice of Kaizen. It is something to embrace because it will expand your learning and improve your Kaizen practice.

The Japanese terms that one hears during Kaizen with Shingijutsu reveal a characteristically Japanese way of conceiving and expressing things. Even words comprised of just two characters can reflect visual concepts, metaphors, wisdom from history, stories, folklore, customs, and so on. Language that expresses the human condition in everyday life and living is a central part of Kaizen and of flow production. Both are alive and evolving to create a better future for humanity, one step at a time.

Efforts made by Western (English-speaking) industrialists to create flow production methods prior to 1950 lacked the basic completeness required to create material and information flow company-wide and were unable to evolve as times changed. They struggled to expand flow across the enterprise and succumbed to reversals to old practices under new managers.

Perhaps language is more important than we realize. English lacks the fullness and richness of language compared to Japanese in the context of situation, knowledge, understanding, and improvement of people, production, and management. We urge you to accept and learn from the Japanese terms used in Kaizen.

NOTES

What did you learn from this chapter?

What will you put into practice?

PART II

DIFFERENTIATION

*Don't teach! Help teams
discover on their own.*

CHAPTER 3

PERSONAL RESPONSIBILITY AND COMPETENCY

What differentiates Shingijutsu? There are three distinguishing characteristics: Vision and Individual Responsibility; Teaching Competency and Style; and an Effective Learning Model for "Making People." The first two are discussed in Chapter 3 "Personal Responsibility and Competency;" the last, in Chapter 4 "Making People."

Individual Responsibility

There is in each Shingijutsu sensei the sense of a grand purpose, of being part of a noble vision and of belonging to an extraordinary legacy. They are taught to be worthy of this inheritance, which motivates a heightened personal responsibility for his actions in pursuit of improving the human condition.

Incumbent on each Shingijutsu sensei, therefore, is the personal responsibility to learn every nuance of flow production and then to inculcate this knowledge in others. Being trained by a Shingijutsu sensei means accepting the same mantle of accountability. One of the original sensei said it this way: "Once you understand flow production, it is your responsibility to apply it and to teach it to others." Being trained also means that you have become part of a highly selective group.

Teaching Competency

Shingijutsu's senior sensei are exceptional people. Not only do they run the company, but they also continue a demanding schedule of leading Kaizens with clients all over the world. Recognizing the critical need to transmit the unadulterated content of flow production to next-generation sensei, Shingijutsu's leadership created the position of Jutsu Shu, literally, the keeper or owner of the technology, art and practice, and granted plenipotentiary authority to the person who occupies this position.

The Jutsu Shu's authority is earned through the respect of his colleagues (and clients) for his wisdom and knowledge, for his many accomplishments, for his teaching ability, and for his discipline. This organizational entity is treated reverently within Shingijutsu.

All of Shingijutsu's sensei are expected to be experts in the Shingijutsu Production System. With subject matter expertise a prerequisite, a Shingijutsu sensei's competency is colored by his teaching style and collateral knowledge and experience. All sensei are trained to obey the rule, "Do not teach." Instead, a sensei is taught to turn questions around into self-study assignments that will lead the questioner to discover, hence, own, the answer and new knowledge on his own. The best sensei employ multiple techniques to motivate and illustrate their points.

Starting with the deeply-held belief that "you cannot learn Kaizen from a book," a sensei may act out or pantomime a role (sometimes assuming the role of a product or customer); sketch symbols and diagrams on a flip chart; invoke a familiar analogy to the team's situation; make bold corrections on a team's map, chart, or layout; become a stand-up comic to show the humor in something; or sing or recite a relevant song or literature passage.

These strategies may be used to goad a team into action or to review the progress that the team has made. During a 3P (Production Preparation Process) workshop, the sensei does not hesitate to get his hands dirty first to encourage others to do the same, to try new approaches, and to not be afraid of failing. Scolding occurs most frequently to a managers or team member who not do as sensei asks, or when a team does not "dive in" to a task.

Another element of teaching style is the degree to which a sensei takes a "hard" or a "soft" approach to facilitating Kaizen. One approach has been called "scary-style" Kaizen, and the other called "human-style" Kaizen. The approaches are analogs of the two strategies for applying force in Japanese martial arts. The hard method (goho), which we termed "tough love" earlier, involves the direct application of force to counter an opposing force; it could be a direct attack (lunge) or the deflection of an opposing attack (parry). The soft method (juho) involves the indirect application of force, for example, to either avoid or redirect the opposing force, often letting the attacker slip by before adding force to the attacker's limb to unbalance or throw him. The styles complement one another, and in Kaizen the expert sensei will use some of each style – scary and human – as befits the situation.

Figure 3-1 Sensei scolding a manager.

A final differentiating attribute of a Shingijutsu sensei is his innate sense of his students' learning progress. There are really no formal tests or evaluations for determining when an organization is ready to move from basic, to intermediate and then to advanced concepts of the Shingijutsu Production System. You must trust the sensei to tell you when you are ready. If asked, the sensei will bluntly tell the organization, "You are not ready yet." "I want you to go back to basics and show me that you fully understand them." Here is an example that amplifies this point.

One of Shingijutsu's clients became enamored of a software package that would automatically create material and information flow diagrams from data in the material requirements planning (MRP) system. To the dismay of the Kaizen Promotion Office (KPO), automating the mapping process would remove an essential practice – hand-drawing material and information flow diagrams – that Kaizen teams needed in their education. But, support for acquiring the expensive software package was growing among the other managers who at the time had only superficial contact with Shingijutsu and flow production. Things came to a head when the director of the Kaizen Promotion Office asked the Shingijutsu sensei for his opinion at a leadership meeting. The sensei replied, "You are not yet ready for this level of automation; when you are, you will realize that you don't need it."

NOTES

What did you learn from this chapter?

What will you put into practice?

CHAPTER 4

MAKING PEOPLE

Shingijutsu is perhaps best known for helping its clients produce their products and services with dramatic increases in safety, quality, and efficiency. Below this, however, lies Shingijutsu's distinctive advantage in what it calls "making people." Why is "making people" so important? Because it is the leadership and collective intellect of an organization's people – their theoretical knowledge ("know what"), their practical experience and skills ("know how"), their system understanding ("know why"), and their motivation and creativity ("care why") – that innovate and deliver the products and services that satisfy customers and accrue profits for investors. In turn, this success reinforces the fulfillment of the team members in a virtuous cycle.

"Making" people means educating, training and coaching people – team members – to achieve extraordinary results. In this chapter, continuing with more of the factors that differentiate Shingijutsu, we expand on Shingijutsu's action-oriented learning methodology.

Preconditions and Preparation

Leadership is prerequisite to making people. Before starting an engagement, Shingijutsu extracts three commitments from leadership:

- Leaders must actively participate in Kaizen activities;
- Leadership must establish a fully-staffed Kaizen Promotion Office to support Kaizen activities across the organization; and
- Improvement must not result in layoffs.

Shingijutsu also has a long planning horizon. Once the dates of Kaizen engagements are laid out and booked for a year, Shingijutsu expects the client to honor the plan; doing so is another dimension of leadership commitment.

Next, selected leaders and associates are sent to Japan for one week to participate in a "full immersion" Genba Kaizen Seminar, which begins with one day of training followed by two days on the shop floor. More recently, genba Kaizen seminars have been successfully held at clients' locations in the United States. More than one participant has called the seminar "grueling." It is here that the wisdom of Kaizen starts to either awaken the imaginations of the client's people or stiffen resistance to change. Some employees, usually leaders, resent being treated as students and rebel at Shingijutsu's teaching methods; these people are usually sent home.

Then comes preparation that is directly related to an upcoming Kaizen. The challenge and goals are set; appropriate Kaizen team members and a team leader are chosen; and then the team undertakes to collect relevant data. To cap off the preparation, which may take one or two days or as much as one or two weeks, a member of the Kaizen Promotion Office delivers training to new Kaizen team members.

These preconditions and preparations are for the client's own benefit; they help ensure that the client will grow to become one with Shingijutsu's Kaizen principles.

Learning Culture

An important facet of Shingijutsu's teaching methodology is deeply rooted in how the Japanese culture treats interpersonal relationships between senior and junior persons. In the context of education, a senior student is senior to all students who started their education and training after him, or, by virtue of other background experience, a senior student may outrank a junior student (for example, team leader vs. team member). The distinctions of senior and junior have more to do with relevant experience than age.

A senior student owns the pivotal responsibility for indoctrinating junior students in the cultural aspects of the school or organization, for example, its manners, work ethic, virtues and philosophy. Junior students have the responsibility to respect their seniors and to afford senior students the opportunity to learn leadership skills. In turn, senior students are expected to lead by example and to encourage the junior students. Some senior students may also teach formal classes under the watchful eye of the instructor. Translating these behaviors and responsibilities to Shingijutsu's learning culture, we can begin to understand the hierarchical relationships among sensei that terminate with the Jutsu Shu as the most senior sensei at the top. We can also appreciate more about the relationship that a sensei is attempting to encourage between an apprentice and him. We will see these behaviors in the case studies included in Chapters 5, 6, and 7.

At the end of an education and training experience, students are customarily awarded a certificate of graduation that proclaims a level of achievement or mastery. The governing body, which grants this document, certifies that the student has satisfactorily fulfilled all of the requirements commensurate with the stated achievement level. Although Shingijutsu has trained thousands of people in genba Kaizen and 3P, the company has only recently developed a certification procedure with accompanying documentation for its students. The certificate, called *menkyo kaiden* in Japanese, carries Shingijutsu's approval for the bearer to teach Shingijutsu's methods on his or her own without the presence of a senior sensei.

Observation Is Learning

Another part of Shingijutsu's learning model involves training people to strengthen their powers of observation. As expected, the training involves practice at the genba, where real work is done. The sensei picks a strategic vantage point, draws an imaginary circle on the floor, and invites the student to stand in the middle of this circle and to turn on all of her senses. The student is then asked to sketch the scene and write down everything that she senses, paying particular attention to things that seem abnormal or out of place. These could include a loud noise, a gathering of people, smoke or a bad smell in the air, congestion in material flow, trash strewn about the floor, an equipment breakdown, people wandering around looking for tools, materials or documents, a bin of defective parts, a stock out, excessive transportation, an unsafe practice or condition, or an operator performing non-ergonomic motions.

Maybe the genba is characterized by chaos and piles of inventory or overloaded in-boxes of work orders, there being no visual sense of an orderly sequence of work nor visual information about the current state of production compared with the customers' daily quota (i.e., takt time). Maybe the observer sees people waiting, or watching a machine work, or daydreaming. Maybe the observer detects that the people are not enthusiastic about their work and that they lack "shiny" eyes. When doing this, the observer will also look for things that are upsetting the harmonious interaction among people, material, information and machines. The observer will also want to keep in mind the four priorities of the genba: safety, quality, productivity, and morale.

When the student returns to the sensei to report her observations, he will point out some things that she has missed. The sensei will ask the student to think about and list all of the kinds of abnormalities that might be observed at a genba, and then return to the genba to observe again. As a prospective student, you should understand that the sensei has in mind that there are 500 or so different abnormalities that might be sensed; they are comprised of the "classical" seven kinds of waste ("muda") plus 493 others. This number, of course, is a metaphor for a large number of things. Try the exercise at your genba!

A more formal approach to "observation as learning" occurs during the week-long, Genba Kaizen seminar conducted by Shingijutsu in Japan and, recently, in the United States. As a condition of engagement, Shingijutsu requires that the leadership and Kaizen Promotion Office staff of a new client attend these sessions. Day 1 features instruction and practice in how to observe and quantify work at the genba using a stopwatch and how to create standard work. During days 2 through 4, the students put their newly acquired knowledge to work in a real factory environment.

Day 5 (when in Japan) involves a plant visit and a tour of a museum. This day reinforces observation is learning, as students see firsthand a world-class factory as well as the power of innovation to drive industry dominance. Over the course of the seminar, students learn how to identify muda (waste), take time data correctly, and prepare and analyze standard work charts, standard work combination sheets, yamazumi charts, Kaizen target sheets, and the Kaizen newspaper. Students are now ready to return to their home organizations and participate effectively in genba Kaizen, where, through practice and further education by sensei, they will continue to learn and grow.

Practice Is Learning

The root *jutsu* in Shingijutsu connotes art or technique gained through practice. For example, reading – a passive involvement – has about a nine percent retention rate; whereas, practicing the real thing – an active involvement – has about an 80 percent retention rate. Simulation and role playing, both active involvements, are not far behind this level of retention in the learning pyramid. But, for practice to be effective, it must be safe and free of threats or apprehension. Shingijutsu sensei have long recognized this phenomenon, and they confront it frequently in their work with teams.

As we will see in the three case studies described in Part III, at least one team in each of the client organizations wanted to shy away from actual practice. Other symptoms of apprehension come in the form of questions asked by team members: "How do I do this?" "What tools should I use when?" "Where is the roadmap of activities that I must follow?" "How can I get help?" "How will I be evaluated?" "How can I be expected to undertake these new activities and still fulfill my present work responsibilities?"

These "how" questions are an attempt by people to deflect change and improvement. To eliminate the very large anxiety that Kaizen will uproot jobs, Shingijutsu requires an advanced promise from the leadership of each client organization that no jobs will be lost because of Kaizen. At the genba the sensei's response starts with encouragement and gentle coaxing: "Please just start taking action; Get your hands dirty and don't be afraid to fail; Don't worry, there is no right way, so you can't make a mistake or fail; Trust me, you won't do anything that will hurt either you or the organization."

Practice is learning has the following features. The sensei, in consultation with leadership and working through the Kaizen Promotion Office, sets challenges for the organization. Kaizen teams of knowledgeable employees discover answers through creative problem-solving, prototyping, simulation, and practice. Only in rare cases, where a slow team may need priming, does a sensei suggest ideas. Work processes keep evolving incrementally; small changes, experiments, moonshining, ever more realistic simulations and practice, and reflection and correction become a way of life (Kaizen forever). The Kaizen coached by a Shingijutsu sensei creates a safe environment.

One activity where many teams need more practice is creative problem-solving, which involves finding root causes of factors that inhibit safety, quality, or productivity, and then generating multiple solutions by identifying functional analogies within nature.

Next a Kaizen team sorts through newly proposed concepts by applying a combination of logic and hands-on trials called "trystorming." Feedback is two-way: the sensei coaches and instructs, and the Kaizen teams replay their learning and progress for validation by the sensei. Behind the scenes some team members are "moonshining," rapidly developing prototypes for the new concepts; indeed, some moonshiners really do work through the night preparing prototypes for their teams to use the next day. At first three-dimensional prototypes are created from easily worked materials at-hand such as: cardboard, foam board, wood, CREFORM® tubes, Lego® bricks, paper, tape, glue, string, wire, etc.

Figure 4-1 Kaizen team members quickly turning ideas into practice.

As the team gains practice through experimentation and simulation, the prototypes are evolved and become more real. The next level of prototypes progress from functional spare parts to development hardware and processes, and then to production hardware and processes. During Kaizen, a team's report at the end of the fourth day occurs at the genba, where the team stages as realistic a demonstration (or simulation) as it can of the improved process, product or service. Throughout Kaizen, the sensei encourages Kaizen teams to develop million-dollar ideas, but not million-dollar solutions. The sensei, like a good orchestra conductor, insists on practice and more practice: "If you practice something 9,000 times and pay attention, you will learn something each time."

30-40-30 Rule

Because of human nature, "making" people does not produce uniform results across an organization. Shingijutsu identifies the progression of people development by the 30-40-30 Rule.

This rule of thumb holds that about 30 percent of the people in an organization will be early adopters and believers in Shingijutsu's methods; that about 40 percent of the people will convert to the new methods after some more coaching; and that the remaining 30 percent of the people will resist the new methods. Whether the percentages are exact is immaterial to the main point of the rule: do not spend additional time trying to convince the naysayers, or you will send a message to the supporters that they are less important to the future of the organization than the resistors are. In fact, after helping the naysayers overcome their objections, for an appropriate length of time, you must discipline them and perhaps even remove them from the organization.

NOTES

What did you learn from this chapter?

What will you put into practice?

PART III

GENBA KAIZEN LESSONS

You have to go back to zero. Put yourself under dire circumstances to think differently.

CASE STUDIES

Many people think that flow applies only to production work. This is grave error that limits its reach in organizations. The following Chapters recount three case studies of Shingijutsu-Kaizen with a hospital, an aircraft engine maintenance organization, and an office furniture manufacturer. You will read examples of Kaizen applied to different types of work both on and off the shop floor. These "live-action" accounts reveal deep insights into Kaizen, how it is taught by Shingijutsu sensei, and what Kaizen team members learn.

Each case study begins with an overview, the Kaizen teams that were formed and the processes to be improved, behind the scene insights from the sensei, and a summary of the Kaizen.

Please pay close attention to the sensei's instructions. These are treasures from which you will learn much about the culture of Shingijutsu and the workings of Kaizen. Also pay close attention to how Kaizen humanizes the workplace.

CHAPTER 5

HOSPITAL KAIZEN

Shingijutsu's efforts to infuse the principles of flow production into a major U.S. hospital have met with enormous success, despite initial skepticism from both internal and external parties. A renowned U.S. authority and author on Lean production stated to the hospital's CEO, who was presenting his plans to a conference on health care, "You will never pull this off in health care; it's just too complex." Internally, several physicians and staff expressed their opposition by the phrase, "Caring for people is not like manufacturing cars." What made the difference was the CEOs unwavering commitment to Kaizen and the continuing assistance and teaching of Shingijutsu sensei.

Overview

This Kaizen was focused on improving three processes: joint mobility therapy for patients recovering from orthopedic surgery, the throughput of the process for sterilizing operating-room implements, and the effectiveness of policy deployment. The Kaizen Promotion Office (KPO) director selected leaders for each Kaizen team and assigned at least one of her people to help each team. The team leaders then selected other team members for their expertise and knowledge.

Each morning began at breakfast with the sensei's review of the schedule with the KPO director, with the interpreter and others shadowing the sensei. With the schedule reviewed, the sensei scolded the group to make sure that they would not repeat some behavior that he found objectionable. Scoldings usually went like this:

> Don't talk, listen! When the sensei tells you something, listen very carefully. Then say "Hai" and go away and think about what he said and why. Come back later and share your observations with the sensei, but never ask him questions.

Often, when you were caught violating these instructions by talking too much, the sensei would give you a withering look and wave one of his arms in a sweeping gesture at shoulder height to signal "Stop it."

Another breakfast discussion centered on the sensei's comparison between the present hospital and a hospital that was affiliated with one of his clients in Japan. After three interactions, the sensei concluded that the hospital in Japan had made no progress. He ascribed the difficulty to lack of leadership commitment. There seemed to be little enthusiasm for Kaizen on the part of leadership, and the sensei's request for the hospital to create a Kaizen Promotion Office had not been acted upon. The comparison between the hospital in Japan and the present hospital was like night to day.

The first activity on the first day was special for the sensei, since he had not visited in two years and wanted to hear an update on overall progress. He attended the CEOs weekly review of the hospital's transformation. The review was held with everyone standing in front of a long wall that was filled with process maps, idea submissions, and charts of data documenting the progress of each directorate's improvements. After all department heads had reported, the CEO made summary observations. Then, the sensei offered his comments.

He was clearly pleased by how far the organization had come, but he was critical of the organization's understanding of material and information diagrams and its use of the term "value stream map" to describe them. His argument was as follows: "Where's the value? I can't see flow on a static map. All I see is waste. You should call this a muda (waste) diagram." Sensei said, "I tried to explain this concept to the people at MIT, but they called it the value stream, even though it doesn't show value-adding flow." He also pointed out that the date was missing, "This was the current state when?," and that if people are in motion, then that must also be shown. Finally, he said that the organization must attend to material flow first before information flow. Here was a prime example of a Shingijutsu sensei not hesitating to correct anyone in the organization; in this case, the CEO, the COO and all the directors.

Once the CEOs weekly review concluded, the sensei started his round-robin genba tours of each team's staging areas and work locations. Each day brought at least two visits to each team; at 4 p.m. the teams would assemble in an auditorium and review their learning and progress for the sensei, the CEO, the sponsors, and the KPO. The auditorium review was not held on Monday afternoon, because several team members were receiving training in genba Kaizen. Normally, such training would be accomplished ahead of time in preparation for the Kaizen. On Thursday afternoon, the review became a genba tour of the individual team locations to observe simulations of how the improved processes would work.

Figure 5-1 Sensei standing on a table to instruct the Kaizen team in an animated and dramatic way.

Patient Joint Mobility Team

At their first meeting, the team leader explained the team's purpose to the sensei. Studies have shown that the speed and completeness of a patient's recovery after orthopedic surgery for joint or hip replacement are favorably influenced by a regimen of joint mobility exercises. Currently, a physical therapist creates mobility charts for each patient and helps the patient conduct the joint mobility exercises appropriate to his or her state of recovery. However, during the swing shift, when the physical therapist isn't there, no joint mobility exercises are done. The team's aim is to enable the swing shift nurses to continue the joint mobility exercises. One abnormality is that the current recovery state of a patient is not well documented and known by either the staff or the patient. Another is that some patients do not want to engage in mobility exercises and are given the option to decline them.

Sensei gave the team the following instructions. He said "I want you to:"

- Validate your purpose and targets.
- Observe and study the genba very closely. What is the need? What is the struggle? Is it time, or therapy time, or patients' time, or money? Make a partial list of reasons and then go to the genba; you do not have to know everything beforehand.
- Charts sometimes lie or are unreliable. Why? When there is no standard, variation occurs.
- Create a work sequence down to the detail of the activities that hands must follow. People at the genba may know the order of activities, but why don't they follow this order all the time? In golf, you may watch someone play and think that you can mimic the motions that you see. But you can't, if you don't know the detailed sequence of movement.
- Make sure that man, motion, machine, and money are all moving in a flexible manner.
- Determine how many patients you must serve in a day. They are your source of income. If the number is variable, how do you adjust? If there are no patients, what happens?
- Try to identify muda. Do you know what muda is? The Japanese word decomposes to mu "no" and da "money."
- We interpret muda as anything that a customer will not pay you for.
- Look at your process. Which parts generate money and which don't? Material and information flow diagrams show the "no-money" areas. Look for the muda.
- Go back to basics and restudy them. The hospital has been at this for three years, and there is a tendency to lose sight of the basics. Recall the reasons for doing Kaizen: eliminate muda, defects, safety problems, inventory, wasted space, patients waiting outside offices while wet, sleep-deprived doctors, nurses moving like bees in a hive, and so on. We've improved many things, but there is still more muda.
- Keep thinking about the things that do not make money, and reduce them by one half each year.

- Use standard work combination sheets. Breakdown work into small time increments, seconds if necessary. Make the hand sequence the smallest increment and define this sequence like a music score, in which the notes are really instructions for where to place your hands.
- Define the level of standard work needed; that is, level 1-4.
- Don't focus on problems (mondai). Instead, focus on what's normal and what's abnormal. When you see an abnormality, work quickly to push it to the normal state.

During the sensei's first tour of the genba (the orthopedic recovery floor in the hospital), he had more observations for the team:

- Your charts are deficient. They are not numbered or dated.
- Your charts are a guide for others to help patients with the mobility events that they are capable of doing. Mistake-proof the charts by using pictures that show levels of exercise, key motions, and patient progress.
- Show the progress sequence in sketches. Don't cut-and-paste pictures from Microsoft's ClipArt. In Japan, people create emoticons to communicate.
- Confirm targets with all team members.

At the next visit with the team, the sensei inspected the team's process map and had the following comments:

- You need to create more process step details for your map.
- What do doctors, nurses and assistants do? If they do something to the patient, then this becomes part of the process.
- Define how you make money. Then look at your processes and see which steps are muda. You cannot charge money for muda.
- The mobility chart is our key information. We want both staff and patient to have visibility of it. Note that it doesn't show time.
- For your process mapping, use you own cartoons, not computer-generated art.

- Do not write too much English; it is not a compact language for conveying ideas. Instead, draw cartoons to convey messages in pictures.

We returned to the genba, where the sensei drew an imaginary "observation circle" on the floor, literally pulled a team member into the center, and instructed him to record and sketch his observations. What did the observer see?

Figure 5-2 A team member standing in the observation circle.

- People congregating in the hall (perhaps a stand-up shift meeting).
- People moving about in apparently random fashion.
- All equipment, except for computer stations in the walls, rolls on wheels.
- When a wall computer station was in use, the pull-down desk top caused the user to stand partially in the hallway.
- Equipment, including two empty beds, was parked on both sides of the hallway, thus restricting movement down the corridor.

- Each patient's room had an Andon-like system of semaphores to alert a visitor of a condition within the room (e.g., doctor examining patient).
- One patient's call light was on.

The sensei noted that the philosophy of the observation circle is to pay attention to all of your senses.

We also watched a patient knee-joint mobility Kaizen, in which a patient was strapped into a walker with the aid of a safety belt and then directed to walk the distance, and return, from the bed to the doorway of the room. The therapist had a difficult time attaching the safety belt while the patient stood still, holding onto the walker. This was an improvement opportunity.

Figure 5-3 Patient and hospital workers struggling.

While on this tour, the sensei diverted us into the supply replenishment room for the floor. The replenishment system had been the subject of an earlier Kaizen and had been overhauled to create a visual, two-bin system that by all accounts from users was working well. In the basement the main distribution source for this and other supply rooms had been organized into a proper supermarket, which featured a visual address for each stock item (equivalent to a street name and house number), the maximum quantity to be stored at each location, and a FIFO (first-in, first-out) storage configuration.

At the 4 p.m. team leaders' meeting on the second day, the team leader presented the Kaizen target progress report. The Kaizen team had identified the following abnormalities related to quality:

- Number of patients who can't verbalize their current state of rehabilitation progress.
- Number of patients who are not receiving the full complement of mobility events that they are capable of performing.
- Amount of time that the registered nurse and the physical therapist have difficulty understanding the patient's appropriate mobility exercises.
- Number of instances when the patient's chart doesn't reflect reality, because information hasn't been updated.

The team also presented its mobility charts, and was told by the sensei that they are improving, but he still wants to see fewer English words on them. Finally, the team showed its "Process-at-a-Glance Chart," which contained an impressive amount of detail for just one day's work. This chart was broken down into enough detail to illustrate the steps required for the swing shift nurses to follow. The steps were visual and easy to understand by the nurses, who had been reluctant to take on joint mobility exercises for fear of injuring the patients. One of the ideas was to place a colored-coded adhesive dot on a sketch of the relevant joint in the patient's mobility chart to indicate the appropriate level of exercise. The sensei told the team that it was doing well.

On the third day, the sensei focused on the team's Process-at-a-Glance chart. The team had been working on inserting in this chart instructions that would help both the nurse and the patient understand the patient's condition. The sensei gave the following direction:

- In the "Manual" boxes, show detailed movements, as fine as the finger level, if necessary.

- In the "Gauge" boxes, include what you see, for example, negative symptoms from actions. What other measurements and observations are important?

- Fill out one column (process step) at a time.

- Show either the patient's motion or the therapist's motion. If you show the therapist's motion, don't show the patient eating, for example.

- The real value comes from the therapist's work; show this.

- Use "stickies" (3M Post-It® notes) for drafting, then transfer your work to a permanent Process-at-a-Glance chart. Quick and plain is better than slow and fancy.

- At the end of the day, take a copy of the chart home and sleep on it next to a pen. Whatever comes to you in the middle of the night, jot it down.

- Remember that the purpose of this chart is to define for your process steps the "5W's and 1H" (What, Who, Why, When, Where, and How) and to show the "5M's" (Man, Method, Measurement, Material and Machine).

- "Steal" ideas and concepts from other Kaizen teams. In Japan we say, "May I borrow this?," with stress on the word borrow. When it comes time to return 'this,' we tell the lender, "You gave 'this' to me."

- Use "moonshine" to rapidly prototype concepts. Moonshine refers to making alcohol illegally in a hidden place under the light of the moon. The activity is done to avoid paying an alcohol tax to the government, so moonshining occurs secretly without permission. It's okay to prototype concepts in this manner for the hospital.

Later at the 4 p.m. team leaders' meeting, the team leader reported that their concept will increase a patient's joint mobility events from two to a consistent three each day. She also shared the sponsor's challenge to hold a go/no-go safety event before assigning anyone who is not a physical therapist to the third event. The sensei stated his desire to see the simulation of the new procedures, and he also had the following comments to make about the Process-at-a-Glance chart:

- It's good that you started from the Process-at-a-Glance chart.
- Show the provider's activities, not the patient's activities.
- Make sure that all of the different kinds of activities are shown.
- Use numbers and even pictures to label the process steps.

Because of an overnight snowstorm, the fourth day started late and many team members were out doing substitute assignments to keep the hospital running. The annual Christmas party was also impacted by the storm, although a few team members had dressed in party costumes – to the delight of our sensei. One costumed woman on the Policy Deployment Team, which was meeting directly across the hall from where the Patient Mobility Team was convened, particularly caught the sensei's eye and gave him an idea. She was dressed as a Santa's elf, complete with a pointed red hat that had white fuzzy trim around the base. He had just come from visiting the Patient Mobility Team, which was struggling with how to respond to patients who did not want to receive mobility therapy.

He counseled the team to "think about the meaning of the service we are providing to make patients happy (kando)." The sensei coached the make-believe elf about his plan, which was to have her burst in on the Patient Mobility Team pretending that she was a physical therapist encountering a patient who was reluctant to receive mobility therapy. He asked her to take a very positive, forthright and enthusiastic approach when she entered the room. With the element of surprise on her side, she effervesced to the mobility team, "Okay, it's time for your mobility exercise. Get up, get up, and let's get going." There was great laughter by all over the sensei's ploy, but the message was clear. Later that day the Patient Mobility Team leader reported that the team had tried this approach on a real patient, and it had worked.

On the afternoon of the fourth day, the team leaders meeting is replaced by a simulation at the genba. The first order of business for the Patient Mobility Team was to observe the Orthopedic Surgery Recovery Floor from the vantage point of an imaginary circle on the floor. We saw that everything appeared to be normal: no unnecessary steps, all equipment on wheels, quiet and not chaos, and no visible andon warnings. The team demonstrated a pre-event decision tree that it developed to determine the eligibility of the patient for mobility exercise. The sensei asked the team to keep studying customer satisfaction and spirit.

Finally, at the close-out session on the fifth day, the sensei had these observations for the team:

- Your task has been difficult, because the flows of patients and caregivers are mixed. You must focus on the activities of the caregivers.
- Your Process-at-a-Glance chart has gotten better, and it shows good artistry.
- On Tuesday you discovered that you had misinformation. Then you went to the floor and redesigned the process after studying each detailed step, including the motions of feet, legs and hands.
- For patients, oral communication with the right attitude is the most important thing: "Merry Christmas, let's get up and move!" If you can make patients happy, one-half of their illness will be cured.

Sensei said: "This week you did great work. I want you to continue. Keep working on your approach for talking to patients."

Policy Deployment Team

The team leader explained to the sensei the results of a center-wide staff survey of policy compliance. A majority of the staff was unaware of the policies mentioned in the survey. Of those who were aware of the policies, a high percentage admitted to not following them.

The sensei explained that policy deployment is called "hoshin." "Ho" means direction and "shin" means needle – in this context, think of it as the needle of a compass. The word hoshin refers to the pointing direction, where the needle points. He continued:

- Policies are guidelines that must be adhered to. I want you to define the adjectives that modify the policies of concern to you, for example, safety policy or patient care policy.

- In your case, you need SIQMI (systematic integration of quality, material and information) – a system of standard work that supports your process. You must understand what a policy is and the sequence of steps to follow in its development and deployment.

At the second meeting, the sensei critiqued the Policy Deployment Team's process map (which showed process flow analysis of activities and interactions by functional disciplines):

- You show the flow of communication and training, but where is the material flow? Without showing the material flow, you haven't got a valid map.
- Show the material flow first (in the direction of left to right), then the information flow (in the direction of right to left).
- I can't understand your map, because there is too much writing on it. What does it say?
- Some things are missing from your map, for example, a policy. Print out a policy and make it an object.
- Show its shape, what it tastes like, its mother, who uses it and drinks it.

Starting from the premise that most Americans don't read policies, and that policies come from people who don't understand policy, the sensei continued:

- You must design a policy so that it's easy for a 9-year old to follow.
- It must be visual and show what is normal and what is abnormal. Include timing. Use all of your senses to check the policy.
- Minimize writing. Try to replace words by cartoons.
- You must have SIQMI (Systematic Integration of Quality, Material, and Information) before hoshin. For example, "Just in Time" is a SIQMI. Hoshin followed later.
- Try to visualize your flow.

- Make sure that each team member understands your purpose.
- A policy must be apolitical.
- If a policy isn't working, is the direction faulty or is the compass needle faulty?
- What is the quality, quantity and timing of the policy? Does the policy interfere with processes? You will see wasted cost from a bad policy.
- How is policy deployment checked at each process step? Are there go/no-go gauges that tell when something is wrong or abnormal? When this happens, is an Andon signal sent to stop the process?

The next day the Policy Deployment team showed the flip charts on which it had captured the lessons from yesterday. The team had identified two safety-related policies that needed to be rolled out: a safety policy for patients and a policy for the care of psychiatric patients. The sensei gave more instructions:

- A written policy is very vague. It is important to give a policy visibility. Make it tangible.
- A policy shouldn't be paperwork. Is what's on paper the policy? Do you have to read it to understand it?
- I want you to think about making a policy without paper.
- Think about the function of the policy. Don't convey it verbally. Instead, create a shape of the policy and a way to convey the shape.
- Many policies are created without the consensus of the people. Think about practice areas where people can learn new policy.
- A policy symbol may show the idea of a policy but not its details. Perhaps you use a cartoon.
- Think of policy as a product for which you need a production process. You must do moonshining – I know that you understand about 3P.
- If policy is a new product, how do you sell it to your customers? Suppose that policy is a box; what design of the

box will attract customers? For example, why is the Coke bottle shaped the way it is?

- You have to see something that you cannot see.
- The solution must be very simple. Make a small object or card as a prototype. I made a card that says: "#1 means to lead innovation and to be the industry leader."
- Establish standard work and revise it. Kaizen is like the spiral on a barber pole.

The sensei then asked one of us to describe the concept of policy to the team. Here is the explanation:

- You have to become the policy.
- Leaders' behaviors must exemplify the policy.
- It must be obvious when the policy is not being followed; an Andon light should signal the abnormality.
- When someone is not following the policy, the culture must support correction.
- Policy deployment is behavior based. For example, a team member should not walk by a piece of paper on the floor without stooping to pick it up.

At the afternoon team leaders meeting, the leader of the Policy Deployment Team reported that the team is trying to create a standard approach to policy, because of recent events in which people were either unaware of a policy or didn't follow it. The sensei sympathized that this team's product is very difficult. He challenged them to create three-dimensional icons to represent policies and to keep thinking how to best show their product.

The next morning the team showed the sensei a prototype of its patient-safety policy. The policy requires that all patients must wear a color-coded wristband that signifies a condition of concern, for example, allergy or drug sensitivity, do-not-resuscitate instruction, risk of falling. The symbol chosen for the policy was a set of multicolored crayons, each labeled with the appropriate condition; on the floor, wristbands would be stored in a crayon box. The team explained that currently there is a national movement underway to standardize the color coding. Then the sensei challenged the team to describe the policy in only one word, and he suggested that the team use, besides different colors, different shapes and symbols for the wristbands.

Attention then shifted to the psychiatric patient-care policy. The team stated that because psychiatric patients are hard to interact with, caring for them is especially difficult. After reviewing the outline of the team's proposed policy, the sensei responded about the need to simplify:

- You say "Assess the Patient." What do you mean by assessment?
- You say "Keep them Safe." What does this mean? Try to visualize and see what you need to pay extra attention to.
- You have identified two approaches. Why are they important?
- Your policy needs more work. It is too vague.

When the sensei next returned, he provided more instruction on policy:

- There are two kinds of policies: One tells people what they must do (beki); the other, what they must not do (bekarazu).
- What people must do is work; what they must not do is create waste.
- Value management often works between these two views, but note that work may also contain waste.
- I want you to sort your policies by these two types.
- Examples of "must not's" are: no money, no space, no crane, no forklift, no big machines, no big cleaning room.
- Use the symbol of a circle with a diagonal line though it to denote "must not do." You will see this symbol in airplane safety brochures. The line runs from upper left to lower right; think of it as the diagonal line in the capital letter N, standing for No.

He explained that 5S is also a policy that is divided in this way: The first two S's, Seiri (Sort, organization) and Seiton (Straighten, set in order) are work that a team member should do; the third S, Seisou

(Sweep), that stands for cleaning is an activity that a team member should not do. In one company, a team member is scolded for cleaning. The key question is, "Why do you have to clean so much?" The bathrooms have signs that say "Don't make a mess;" they don't say "Clean." The sensei then made the point that if people fail to follow a policy, people should feel some kind of pain as a result, for example, a penalty or a fine.

At that afternoon's Leadership Meeting, the Policy Deployment team presented their next attempt to meet the sensei's requirements for policy formulation and deployment. They showed the sensei a revised policy management checklist and shared their learning that the more preparation time put into a policy, the less time will be required for its deployment. They also reviewed the status of their two pilot policy projects. He told the team:

- This is becoming much better.
- The wristbands look good and seem on their way to becoming a federal standard that will be fixed for a long time. Copyright the brochures that you create to explain the policy.
- Instead of the symbol of an egg for your psychiatric care policy, can you find something that moves around, for example, a little fish, a puppy or a kitten? What about a baby that needs to be protected?
- Look for symbols in nature, for example, birds protecting their young. How do cats transport their kittens?
- If you can make your policy a SIQMI (systematic integration of quality, material and information), then top management won't need to have so many policies.
- As I told you last time, try to separate your policies into "Do" and "Do Not" categories.

The next day, Thursday, was impacted by the aftermath of the snowstorm. As a result, the Policy Deployment Team was only partially prepared for the afternoon genba tour, where each team was supposed to simulate or enact its solutions. The sensei's reactions were as follows:

- Planning for a policy and its deployment starts earlier than you show.
- Incorporate 5W1H in your management checklist and planning tool.
- Your management checklist and planning tool should then travel with the process.
- All policies are not equal. The team should develop a sorting algorithm, for example, safety, skill building, new tools and suppliers, risk, intensive or easy.

In response to the sensei's request to see actual examples and not just hear explaining, the team returned to the team room where they had examples of the planning tool, a deployment kit, testing of the kit, feedback to process owners and the sponsor, and transfer of a policy to operations. The sensei requested that the team prepare more visuals for their presentation and also show the Do/Do Not Do list.

On the final day at the close-out meeting, the sensei gave the team his summary:

- The concept of a policy was hard for the team to see at the beginning of the week, but it is now clearer.
- A policy means things that people are supposed to do or not do.
- When an abnormality happens, it means that someone did not follow a policy.
- Policy must become a habit – second nature.
- When a bad habit shows up, you need a consequence, for example, a slap.
- First policy becomes your habit; then it becomes your DNA.

Sterilization Process Team

We met the team that was tasked with improving the throughput of the sterilization process for operating room implements at its staging area. The actual genba was hot, steamy and busy – generally inhospitable to a tour. The sensei began by asking the team members to explain their Process-at-a-Glance chart that occupied a large wall. He was quite pleased by the chart and had a number of comments:

- Under "Process Steps," list nine or so steps (up to 20 steps, if necessary, but not a very large number).
- Describe your purpose, need and datum. Also include QQT (quality, quantity, and timing).
- For each storage location, show the address, the quantity and the first-in, first-out (FIFO) arrangement.
- Show kit carts and their frequency of movement.
- For WIP in the decontamination process, what is the ideal WIP? WIP (work in process) is the number of carts waiting for decontamination. Standard Work in Process (SWIP) should be two; zero is not good, because you need one or two carts waiting so that you can keep replenishing the process.
- Based on time, I want you to check on the causes of variation you see. Identify why and the biggest problem areas.
- Your decontamination process should become more like a chakku-chakku (load-load) line.
- Study more about tools: special tools (called "dogu" in Japanese) unique to the hospital and your process plus commercial, off-the-shelf tools ("kogo").
- See if you can replicate the idea of the Japanese automated toilet in your process. This toilet provides water pulsing and a quick finishing wash followed by an air-drying cycle.
- Do 3P (Production Preparation Process).

Tuesday morning the sensei returned to the team's staging area. Earlier the team had arranged with the Pacific Science Center to set up their traveling science laboratory exhibits on tables around the room in order to inspire the team's creativity. The sensei looked at all of the tables and then went to work to build a bridge from the blocks found at one of the tables. He told the team that the first step was to define the method, which was not defined by the numbers on the blocks but by the sequence of hand actions to be followed. His method was to assemble the blocks horizontally on a sheet of plywood, which would later be pivoted to a vertical position. He asked, "What is the material flow in this example?" It was the arrival of blocks at the assembly or construction site.

Returning to the Process-at-a-Glance chart, the sensei remarked:

- First establish the methods, quality standards and gauges, consumable supplies, and tools – then the machine.
- Don't design the process around the machine; define the machine last.

The sensei then inspected the mocked-up washing station and had more comments:

- Why do you have a wash cart in the first place? Why is there such a big bath?
- Look at the cart's function and then look to nature for better concepts.
- How can you avoid or reduce washing? Washing is not the function; no-washing should be the function.
- Imagine yourself to be the cart going through the wash. Where or what do you need to wash? How long does it take to wash? In this time what gets washed? Where does the spray hit? Exactly where?
- I want you to create two sub-teams – a cart team and a wash team
- The cart team is to define functions and build carts out of tube material that can withstand the hostile environment of your process
- The wash team is to generate and explore seven options for washing concepts. Follow the 10 basic steps of 3P. Breakdown work in small enough detail that muda stands out.
- Try to identify the muda of washing, for example, size of washing machine and excess water usage.

At the end of the visit, the sensei told the team, "I'm not trying to harass you. I'm giving you some knocks for practice, like the cage for batting practice or the bullpen for pitching warmup."

The 4 p.m. team leaders' meeting brought the following comments from the sensei:

- There are so many things to consider, but I want you to focus on the washing process.
- Ask yourselves, why do we have to wash in the first place?
- Who decides what has to be washed? Are we separating things that are basically clean from those that are dirty, or is everything just being washed together?
- Your process has two basic functions: deliver only clean cases and tools to doctors in the operating room; receive only dirty cases and tools from the operating room. Don't mix these functions.
- You need to change your way of thinking about this process.

The next morning at breakfast, the KPO director told the sensei that the Sterilization Process Team was having doubts about its ability to make progress without including the operating room processes and staff. Morale was down and whining was starting to displace motivation. When he met next with the team, the sensei had these instructions that were delivered in stern (scolding) tones:

- I want you to develop a concept for separating clean items from dirty items.
- Proceed without involving the operating room – you don't need them now for what you have to do.
- If you choose a spray for washing, how will you ensure full coverage? Think about putting a person in protective gear inside the washer to observe, or use video cameras.
- Eliminate the ramp (for pushing carts up into the washer); the replacement must be simple. Your ambulance stretcher scissor lift is much too complicated. Perhaps there is an overhead wire.
- Eliminate steam; convert to a chemical process.

- The door to the washer is too wide. You need to improve the design. Think of new ideas for a door that is quick to open and close. Look at a paint line. Consider an air curtain or an air knife.
- Develop a SIQMI so that anyone can perform the washing function.
- Create hanedashi (auto-eject device) so that washed pieces get ejected automatically.
- Sketch your concepts. Make sure that you have seven ways to perform each one.

He concluded the session with a pep talk:

- Explain why the sensei scolded you when give your presentation this afternoon.
- Post the muda chart; show unnecessary cleaning.
- Use wisdom, not money.
- You are all very good, but not good enough.

The team's presentation at the 4 p.m. team leaders' meeting received further advice from the sensei, who did not like the team's strategy of first understanding the answers to the question, "What is washing?"

- Your basics of 3P are still at the kindergarten level.
- I want you to revisit the third S. The third S is Seiso, and you are thinking about washing.
- You should be asking, "Why do we have to wash carts in the first place? Who or what makes carts dirty? How can we avoid making the carts dirty?"
- The normal state must be not making a mess, because when you do, you must clean.
- The carts are not that dirty. You are telling me lies (koshakushi).
- How can we not make carts dirty?
- You must separate clean carts from dirty carts.
- Keep asking "Why?"
- Now the team knows what to do.

The next day the team ran its simulation for the sensei. He offered the following advice:

- Use your imagination to define the process steps. Think of the steps that you go through to bathe. (To punctuate his point the sensei enacted a humorous and animated demonstration of the bathing process.)
- Think about how to create flow through the washer and what could be the pacemaker. For example, one company that has to cure parts in an oven has the oven located overhead (where workers are remote from high temperatures) and the parts are conveyed though the oven on a trolley that is the pacemaker. By the time that the parts exit the oven, they are cured.
- Create a normal state. Fix abnormalities to achieve smooth flow.
- When an abnormality occurs, stop the line. The washing machine needs sensors to signal an abnormality and automatically stop the process (jidoka).
- Ask why many times. Why do carts get dirty and have to be washed? Why do you have to wash the whole frame so many times?
- Go back to the basics. Implement all 10 steps of 3P: functions, people, key words, applicable phenomena from nature, seven ways, moonshining, selected concepts, three-dimensional mockups, simulation, evaluation, repeat.

After the washing simulation, the team showed the sensei a board on which the process for interacting with the operating room and flows of carts were simulated using colored yarn, paper labels, and small objects. The sensei commented:

- Your carts are too big. Consider QQT: quality (what?), quantity (how many?) and timing (when?).
- One-piece flow requires pull. You must pull from the point of delivery.
- You are too stingy with people. Water striders are an important part of a process. (The sensei took this

opportunity to refer to the "Lady Buddha" who has 1,000 arms for helping people.)

- Your process needs to have a store.

At the afternoon genba tour, which replaces the 4 p.m. team leaders' meeting on the fourth day, the sensei was brief with the team:

- You have done a very good job with your Process-at-a-Glance chart, and you have created standard work combination sheets.
- You need to simplify everything. Don't spend a lot of money.
- You haven't done anything about functional details, why things need to be washed.

The sterilization team's presentation to the closeout Leadership Meeting on the fifth day was filled with humility. They had learned many lessons. Perhaps the most important was that they were not as good as they had thought and that they had much more to learn. The team's sponsor also echoed the notion of humility by stating that the team is like a twelve-year old, who has much to learn. The sensei gave the following feedback to the team:

- This team did lots of tasks.
- Their significant result is the Process-at-a-Glance chart.
- The basics of 3P (Production Preparation Process) require a team to first look at the processes, which were not defined. The team worked on designing the processes.
- But the people didn't understand the exact functions of the process activities. They didn't ask the question for each process step, "Why do you do this?" They didn't answer the biggest question, "Why wash?"

Behind the Scenes with Sensei

Our sensei had established a practice with this hospital of spending time with personnel from the Kaizen Promotion Office to elaborate on a jointly chosen topic. On the schedule two hours were allotted for this activity. The topic chosen for this session was "Basics" (kihon). Earlier in the week the sensei told senior leadership that the hospital had been doing genba Kaizen for three years, and it was time for them to move on to the next level after reviewing the basics to make sure that everyone understood what they had done. The sensei said:

> Right now the genka (costs) of this hospital are huge: the numbers of physicians, nurses, staff, supplies, equipment, and buildings. Genka must be reduced. How? Identify and eliminate muda – those costs that are waste. There should be only minimal numbers of doctors and nurses, equipment and so on. You have to figure out what will be the minimum in each case – the ideal state. These are the basics.

It is difficult to visualize the ideal state, because work makes things invisible. Standard work is one way to see. It has three elements:

- Takt time – What must be accomplished in eight hours. By definition Takt is the available working time (say, eight hours) divided by the demand in this period. For example, a nurse has to do preparation; in how many seconds must she do each preparation task to complete the total number of preparations required in her work day?
- Work sequence – Not a random sequence of process activities, but a manual sequence of activities defined to the level of hand and even finger movements. A good analogy is the finger movements for playing the piano according to the notes in a music score.
- Standard Work in Process (SWIP) – The minimum levels of work in process to sustain a continuous flow. There should be only one job waiting and one in process. If there are more than two jobs waiting, then you have an abnormal condition and Muda.

Each team member must have standard work, which is created by preparing the standard work sheet and the standard work combination sheet.

Another basic is how you learn from the sensei. When you ask questions, don't expect straight answers from me. Start by saying, "My opinion is this." I will reply, "Pass" or "Fail." I might also scold you for not knowing better. With this remark, the sensei began to interact with the audience. A participant observed: "A nurse has many tasks to perform, and Takt is the amount of time she has to devote to them. But there seems to be a difference between individual and process Takt times." Sensei replied:

> You know Takt times and can create standard work for the process steps that each individual has to perform. Individuals, including doctors and nurses, have to accept it. Knowing that standard work is basic, it must be practiced and improved. As an example, look at Ichiro's (Suzuki) work: fielding, batting and running for the Seattle Mariners major league baseball team. Can you do what Ichiro does? You need skills and training, and you have to know what kind of training, for example, batting practice in a batting cage. At this hospital we are working on training resources. As one example, there is a fake arm for phlebotomists to practice on while drawing blood. But these people must also go out and work with real patients. Each training area needs a coach, and this is the role of the Kaizen Promotion Office. What is the KPO? It's the Kaizen Coaching Office. In an earlier example, the KPO coach helped a technical expert create standard work for a Code Y response, including timing, sequence, tools and visual controls. In Japan, there is a short brochure that explains what to do when someone is having a heart attack. I have seen people run simulations.

The sensei continued:

> There are many different types of genka (costs); some you can see, some that you can't see. You can call genka Total Cost. Whatever the name, it must be reduced. You can identify genka by categories – man, material, and machine. An important part of basics (kihon) is 5S. Study the third and fourth S's: Seisou (Sweep, cleaning) and Seiketsu (Sanitary or clean). The intent of the first two S's (Seiri - organization, sorting and Seiton - put in order or straighten) is that if you do them well, then you won't need to do the other S's so frequently. I want you to change your 5S charts to reflect this. The first S (Seiri) refers to having what we need when we need it. It is Just-In-Time, and it requires

separating what is needed from what is not needed and getting in the way.

I will use a beer analogy to explain JIT: in Germany the way the beer is poured causes foaming, and people must wait for the bubbles to settle before drinking the beer; in Japan people can drink the beer three seconds after it is poured. The Japanese way is just in time; the German way is just out of time. In baseball Ichiro is famous for running to first base, always one foot faster than the ball. He is very precise, to the point that umpires have stopped watching instant replays of his action. What does he watch and sense to be this precise? In the hospital, the first S in the operating room means quick access – the nurse always has the right tools ready for the surgeon. This is also part of standard work.

In the beginning, there were two S's. Of course, areas must be clean, without dirt, chips or dust, and the engines must be free of even tiny grains of sand. Therefore, we created the third S, Seisou (Sweep, cleaning). The fourth S, Seiketsu (Sanitary, clean), means that after you have cleaned, keep it that way. Think of it as sustaining cleanliness. Separate dirty from clean. The fifth S, Shitsuke (Self-discipline), is common sense – if you don't make a mess in the first place, there is nothing to clean up. These are the basics. There are also other S's, Japanese words that stand for thoroughness, forever (until you die), speed, and so on.

So JIT is the same as the first S: what you want when you need it. The in and out parts of a process are separated. There are minimal worker hours and jidoka is in place, so that an abnormality stops the process automatically. In Toyoda's loom business, the looms operate at 700 motions/minute; but when a thread snaps in a machine, the entire machine stops. Stopping is important – how do we sense an abnormality and then make the process stop?

A participant observed: "I have a personal example to relate about the hospital. When I went for my flu shot this fall, the clinic discovered that my tetanus booster was out of date. They gave me both shots and saved my inconvenience of having to return." The sensei then told that he had blood work done when he first arrived for the engagement. He remarked that this was the fastest and most painless blood work that he had ever experienced.

The sensei continued speaking:

> 5S must be in cartoon form, and you should show it in the "Do/Do Not Do" format that I recommended to the Policy Deployment Team. We used 5S in the new design of patient rooms. A rule derived from the first S, or JIT, is that staff must not leave the room to find needed supplies. Instead, essential supplies are kept in the room. The next rule is that the person delivering supplies must not enter the room; instead, there is a pass through opening so that deliveries can be made from the hall. The orthopedic recovery floor is a very good example of 5S. When things are functioning smoothly, the floor becomes quieter.

The last topic that the sensei talked about before disbanding the session involved the dimensions of kihon (basics). He enumerated three elements:

- Honesty, sincerity
- Humility
- Thoroughness

For thoroughness he used the Japanese word "teti," meaning thoroughly, top-to-bottom, beginning-to-end, head-to-toes, head-to-tail. We spent several minutes talking about humility and not letting pride of accomplishment become a barrier to further improvement. He asked if there is well-known story in English about a person who grows too proud before being humbled by events. We thought of Dickens' *A Christmas Carol*, in which Mr. Ebenezer Scrooge is humbled by the ghosts of Christmas past, present and future in his dreams and then awakes to become a better person who has compassion for others.

Summary

Throughout the engagement it was clear to us that the sensei was practicing "human-style" Kaizen. Perhaps two or three times, however, he did resort to scolding a team that wasn't listening to his advice and, therefore, not making as much progress as he wanted. After one scolding episode the sensei confided in us, "When I scold teams, it means they are doing well. Slap, slap, and they get stronger."

We came to understand the wisdom of Shingijutsu's teaching methodology. After being rebuked by the sensei and swallowing our pride to achieve an appropriate state of humility, we were able to explore the depths of "why" and reach new knowledge. Being able to reflect our new knowledge back to the sensei added to the power of the learning experience.

Certainly, the biggest learning of the week was understanding the sensei's perspectives on 5S. Realizing that we were wrongly interpreting and practicing 5S for many years in our different organizations was a stunning revelation. We shall discuss 5S further in Chapter 8, "Basics."

At the closeout meeting the hospital's CEO had the following to say:

> Everyone did great work, notwithstanding the weather and its consequences to the team members. The connection of patient mobility to our fall prevention program is critically important. I am looking forward to more work on policy deployment; we made a good start, but there is more to do. We should not put in place strange policies. I want especially to thank our sterilization team members for the work they do under less than desirable conditions to keep the operating room always ready with sterile instruments. This week has continued to show how important it is to engage our administration, staff, and people. Thank you, sensei, for being provocative, inspiring, challenging, and reminding us to remain humble. Kando is really about passion.

NOTES

What did you learn from this chapter?

What will you put into practice?

CHAPTER 6

AIRCRAFT ENGINE REPAIR KAIZEN

An MRO (Maintenance, Repair, and Operations) business shares some of the characteristics of a hospital. Customers (insurance carriers) agree to a scope of work and price, but there is always the element of surprise waiting when a component (patient) is disassembled (operated on) and inspected (visual, radiology, biopsy). Repair (patient) loads are unpredictable, yet there is a premium on turnaround time. A receiving dock with piles of boxes containing components to be repaired is the dual of a waiting room filled with patients. Then there are the inevitable emergencies.

For the MRO in this case study, an emergency is an aircraft on the ground (AOG) because of an unscheduled engine removal; for the hospital, an emergency is a patient who has a life-threatening condition. Another interesting parallel is the need to handle clean and dirty components (recovering patients, ailing patients and used operating room implements) under the same roof while avoiding cross-contamination. As we saw with the hospital case study above, the MRO presents a limitless number of opportunities for genba Kaizen.

In this section, we describe the first half of a week-long Kaizen engagement with the aftermarket repair operation of a major aircraft engine manufacturer. The repair operation now reported to a new Vice President, who was a long-time supporter of genba Kaizen and Shingijutsu. The new VP made it a point to visit the site once a day, often unexpectedly, to check progress and talk with his managers and the sensei; the VP was particularly concerned that the teams were not confronted by roadblocks that he could resolve quickly at his level.

Five Kaizen teams were involved: Honeycomb Production Cell, Tag Creation and Compliance, Major Rotating Parts Cell, Machine Uptime, and Shipping and Receiving Cell. After an overview of the engagement, we will describe the sensei's interactions with each team and relate our behind-the-scenes discussions with the sensei.

Overview

The Kaizen was led by a first-generation Shingijutsu sensei, a person trained by a senior sensei. He had been engaged with the client repair operation for five years; his annual visits were relished by the repair operation's management because the sensei accomplished so much within a week's time and gave the organization new targets for the next 11 months. Because the sensei and the authors commuted from different locations to the site, our times together occurred during breaks. We were also able to meet with the sensei a week before the engagement to discuss his perspectives about Shingijutsu. At the kickoff meeting on Monday morning, the general manager made the following remarks:

> We welcome back our sensei and visitors. We know that Kaizen works. In the last year, we have reduced our turnaround time by 25 percent, we have reduced our cost of poor quality, and for the last three months our on-time delivery performance has exceeded 80 percent, an historic high for this operation. I want to emphasize our learning from Shingijutsu: safety first, then quality, then productivity. I wish you all a good week.

Each team then made its opening presentation to the sensei, who took notes and returned comments after each presentation. When the presentations were finished, he had several generic comments:

> I haven't been here for a while. Your VP told me of his dream when he took over his present job. He wants to bring customers to this operation, but first it must be world class. In a world-class plant, there is Just-In-Time everywhere; flow with no stagnation; and each process has the right amount of standard work in process (SWIP). When someone asks "What is the right amount of SWIP for your process," each team member should know the answer. If you put more parts into a cell than SWIP, the cell can't handle the load. To be world class, you need to have a pull system implemented. And, everything must be visual. We need to see how things are running. We need to know how many machines are not running; my guess is that you don't know this information now. Even when you are world class, you have to pay attention to safety, quality/defects, and machine breakdowns.

You have to put systems in place to enforce safety and to prevent defects and machine breakdowns. Once you implement these systems, you should be able to achieve another 50 percent reduction in turnaround time. We will become world class. We will have lots of visitors. This week we have one team working on machine breakdowns (Machine Uptime Team). There is one team (Tag Creation and Compliance) working on defects. The other teams (Honeycomb Production Cell, Major Rotating Parts Cell, Shipping and Receiving Cell) are working on aspects of a pull system. Each team must work on achieving its goals for this Kaizen. It will be great to say at the end of the year that we did many Kaizen and achieved our goals. But to feel this way, we must do everything that we set out to do by the end of this week.

Machine Uptime Team

This team's first presentation to the sensei explained that machine uptime is below the organization's goal and that manufacturing technical service (MTS) is behind on maintenance tickets. MTS supports 335 machines, although the data for machine classification appear to be wrong. The sensei responded:

- I want the team to pick one machine today to work on.
- Instead of repairing a machine after it breaks, look for early indications to warn when the machine is about to go down. For example, a temperature is higher than normal, or a pressure is too low.
- Understand this, then incorporate it into your maintenance plan.
- You need to do a proper ABC categorization of all of your machines.
- You also need to have a fast response system – when a machine does break down, you must do something quickly.

At the 4 p.m. team leaders' meeting, it was evident that the team was struggling. The sensei offered the following advice:

- Look at your A category machines. If they are old, decide whether to continue to use them. Perhaps some will have to be replaced because they are not safe.

- Don't neglect your machines and this decision, or you will end up with machines that won't work well for a long time.

- If a machine is old, there are likely no repair parts for it, no manuals, and no information about who can repair it. It is as though your organization has heart disease – your functioning gets worse and worse, but you don't recognize it until it's too late.

The team leader replied to the sensei, "You just described 50 percent of our equipment." The sensei continued:

- What this team is doing is very important. You might be able to create a great cell, but if there are machine problems, you won't get production.

- Some of your machine problems could be fatal. You need to create a system for predicting machine problems. I used to work for a company that had 3,000 machines and a policy not to do maintenance. As long as the machines were running well, there was no need to do maintenance. But some of the machines started breaking down after six months. It took nine people nine years to cover all 3,000 machines and implement total productive maintenance. For your 335 machines, I would anticipate nine people for one year – it will still be time consuming.

- The moral is that you need a system to monitor running machines and to provide feedback. Then frequency of checkups can be done on a case-by-case basis.

The next morning the team leader reported to the sensei that seven of the operation's most critical machines were down, and that the leader had to deploy his team members to fix them. He was short-handed because some of his mechanics took the day off (it was Election Day) and others were on medical restrictions. The team leader shared tomorrow's plan to focus on the machines in a model cell in one of the critical production areas, and he also stated that his team has focused on closing open maintenance tickets that have environment, health or safety implications. The sensei patiently made the following points:

- At least you know that the reality is far from what it should be.

- You need to get back to basics before attempting Kaizen.

- Look at the daily walk-arounds, on-hand spares for critical machine components, and whether repair instruction manuals exist or not.

- Categorize your machines into A, B, or C categories.

- You also have to decide how to handle old machines that can no longer be fixed.

- Please work on the basics this week.

- Machine preventative maintenance relies on operator walk-arounds that are not what they should be. The culture should be that those who operate the machines have ownership of them.

- The checklist for a walk-around should be easy to use, although it takes a little time to conduct the walk-around.

There was obviously no progress for this team to report to the 4 p.m. team leaders' meeting. The sensei instructed the team leader, "Tomorrow, please have all team members do the work that they are supposed to do."

Tag Creation and Compliance Team

After a repair is completed, the repair operation must submit documentation to support the airworthiness of the repaired part. The documentation for the Federal Aviation Administration is called a "tag;" for the military it is called a "certificate of conformance." The team leader told the sensei that there are mistakes in some of the documents submitted, and that this leads to costly rework that also damages the reputation of the repair operation and delays the preparation of new repair documents. The team stated that its goals are 100 percent data integrity (zero defects), 100 percent first-pass yield, 100 percent standard work, and good visual controls. The sensei directed the team to come up with as many mistake-proofing ideas as possible for the errors, with the goal of 100 percent data integrity every time.

Later at the 4 p.m. team leaders' meeting, the team leader related the team's direction to focus on mistake-proofing and to eliminate the manual creation of documents in favor of using the data available from the computer information system. The sensei said:

- Think of what you do in analogy with a supermarket checkout line.
- You should post all of your documents on your material and information flow diagram at the appropriate locations.
- You also must understand where and when mistakes are made and why (root causes analysis).

The next meeting with the sensei found the team busily working on its material and information flow diagram. He had the following suggestions:

- Once you understand the flow, then ask for IT support.
- Print out all of the documents that you use and attach them to your map. Then look for opportunities to eliminate or combine documents.
- What you need is to have the part and its documentation flow in parallel. At the end, an inspector checks the paperwork to ensure that it was properly filled out. You don't want inspectors to fill out forms.
- Can you create a standard list of repairs? If you can develop a standard list of repairs and it is mistake-proofed, then the mechanic won't pick the wrong repair to do.

The team leader noted that an abnormality occurs when, at the end, the inspector discovers a repair that was done but not called for in the work scope; then the inspector has to remove the extra repair, and this introduces mistakes. There is also sometimes different information in the information system and our manual documenting system. The sensei continued:

- Work on your process first.
- It is necessary for you to implement an interim solution that you can start using on Monday.

- You won't be able to go entirely paperless - some work instructions will need to be printed out, laminated and posted.

That afternoon on his return visit, the sensei saw that the whole team was working busily on laying out documents associated with the process steps. He praised the team and continued with his coaching:

- This is a really nice Kaizen team. Everyone is gathered around working and trying to figure out what to do.
- During Kaizen, it is usually not possible to satisfy everyone 100 percent. But if you find something in common, or a way to automate manual work, then do it. In particular, try to develop mistake-proofing.
- Because of the lead time to produce IT solutions, implement whatever you can to make life easier. Think of it as buying tomatoes – you can buy them individually by the pound or pre-packaged in a bag; do whatever is easier for everyone. Try to find common forms, like bags.
- Automate as much as possible.
- Make something that everyone can use on Monday.

At the 4 p.m. team leaders' meeting, the team leader reported that the team had demonstrated document flow. They now knew what data were populated at each step. They also had learned which data were manually vs. automatically populated. The sensei remarked:

- What your team is doing is good.
- Try to create a long-term solution plus a short-term solution.

Honeycomb Production Cell Team

Honeycomb structures are used for seals between rotating blades and the annular casings in an aircraft engine. The seals are produced in segmented arcs and then brazed onto a ring. To repair a seal, the worn honeycomb elements are first mechanically removed from the ring and new segments are brazed back into place. The teams stated to the sensei there was excessive queue time. When the team members told the sensei their target for turnaround time, he recalled, "This was your goal two years ago. I remember telling you to cut it in half."

That afternoon the team showed the sensei its concept for a "pitch" (heijunka) box for achieving flow. The sensei, less than impressed, commented:

- That's fine, but you have to manage the output, too.

- Plus, there must be critical monitoring points to ensure that the process is operating on Takt. Then add buffering where it can't keep up.

- I know that you are looking at the cell, but you must see the bigger picture on the floor. You can't pull a job in unless you ship a job out.

- A sister organization of yours in the next building uses a number of special carts to monitor production. The carts go around the cell. It's easier to monitor production using carts, because when an empty cart comes back, you know that it's time to induct another one.

- How many parts need to be moving? (The team showed the sensei actual parts, and a discussion ensued to enumerate the data for daily demand of jobs, SWIP, number of honeycomb sections in a job, and number of parts in the brazing furnace at one time.)

- Once you implement a pull system, then focus on abnormal situations. Set a time limit for solving a problem locally, then escalate by using an Andon signal to summon help.

- You must not reject everything now – you need to improve, not throw things away.

- Go to the shop floor and see how things work today. Look at your current state.

- Also go next door to benchmark you sister organization.

The team's presentation at the 4 p.m. team leaders' meeting provoked these comments from the sensei:

- Your sister organization doesn't use your pitch-box concept to achieve pull.
- You need to know your lot size.
- How many pieces do you receive from your customers and how does the lot size compare with the capacity of your equipment?

During his visit with the team the next morning, the sensei said to the team:

- Your processes are too separated to permit one-piece flow.
- It's okay to use boxes of approximately six parts per box, but you have to find a convenient way to move the boxes.
- You must design the solution yourselves. If the solution comes from me and it doesn't work, you will think that I don't know what I'm doing.

That afternoon at the 4 p.m. team leaders' meeting, the team reported on a benchmarking visit to its sister organization, a cause-and-effect diagram of impediments to the sensei's goal of halving turnaround time, and a training gap and WIP analysis of the inspection process bottleneck. Then they conducted a simulation of their proposed pull system, about which the sensei has this to say:

- Within the given times for processing a tray or box, you have to do the work and put it back?
- What happens when the cart's place is empty? Does this signal an abnormal condition?
- You have to show the real flow; otherwise, I can't tell what's going on. I can't see how the boxes are flowing in your design.
- Tomorrow I would like you to show me what the overall flow is.

Major Rotating Parts Cell Team

Major rotating parts in an aircraft engine refer to air seals, hubs, the disks that hold compressor or turbine blades, and drums comprised of stacks of disks that are welded together. Disks are expensive and long-lead items, and not all damaged disks can be repaired. One function of this cell is to determine whether a disk still meets airworthiness requirements. If not, the cell must procure a replacement disk. The goal of this team is to design an efficient cell that will minimize turnaround time. Achieving it will require closer coordination with the team's major customer, an engine overhaul center that disassembles engines and performs some in-house repairs and sends the rest out to specialized repair operations. Part of the team's goal will require not duplicating operations already performed by its customer.

At the kickoff meeting, the Major Rotating Parts Cell team leader explained to the sensei that the disk process takes several weeks to determine whether a disk is airworthy or must be replaced with a new one. About 21 percent of disks sent by customers require replacement; for military engines, 100 percent must be replaced. Replacing a disk creates a major headache for the engine center customer because of the length of time involved. In fact, disk replacement accounts for 80 percent of this repair organization's customer dissatisfaction.

The sensei's first reaction was to request that the team define the flow from engine disassembly at the customer's site to when the repaired or replaced material was back at the customer's site. At the first one-on-one meeting with the sensei, the team leader elaborated: "We have a material and information flow diagram from our customer's engine disassembly process to our cell. In the end, all parts come here, although we do see partial repairs conducted by our customer. The open question is, 'Who should do the repairs?' Our customer believes that they should do what they can, because it will save money. They also believe that we want to repair everything here because that will make more money for us. There are two kinds of repair. The first involves 'severe damage;' the damaged part should be shipped dirty to us. The second is a light repair. Our customer spends a lot of time looking at parts at its site, and there are quite a few engine parts waiting for cleaning. The question of what work should be done here vs. at the customer's site is still unresolved."

The sensei suggested that the team come up with several proposed cell designs and then create a business case to see which ones are affordable. Further, at the 4 p.m. team leaders' meeting, the sensei asked the team to look at how another sister repair operation manages heavy vs. light repairs. He said that this repair operation used to have a mixed model line; they had difficulty achieving flow until they separated light repairs from heavy repairs by creating a separate cell for heavy repairs.

The next morning the sensei discussed cell design and layout with the team:

- There is a rule of 15 in cell design. There should be no more than 15 people, machines and processes in a cell.

- At the location where a part leaves a cell, that's where to situate another cell.

- There was a poor example of cell design at one of your sister divisions. It was a machining cell with 75 automated machines. Never once did this cell run well. Operators had to remove parts from the cell, take them elsewhere to be machined, and then bring them back.

- There is a basic rule of cell design: once a part leaves a cell, it must never come back.

- Your sister repair operation that I mentioned yesterday manages light-to-heavy repairs with the help of three cells, which can be accessed as shown in the accompanying figure.

- Note that once machines are fixed to the floor, your flexibility for rearrangement is gone.

- I want you to think about what you would do, if you could have one more machine. What would it be? How would it improve the cell?

- You will also have to make decisions on what to do with older machines. If you continue to rearrange existing machines around this operation, you will continue to experience machine problems and breakdowns.

- You need to continue to look at better ways and new technology for doing things. For example, when we created the Honeycomb Cell, we tried to eliminate cranes. But the turning machine had a very heavy fixture. We asked, is there a machine that doesn't need such a heavy fixture?

Yes, it's an end mill. So, we experimented with the end mill in the stators cell and decided to purchase three new end mills for the Honeycomb Cell.

- If I don't say anything, most teams will just rearrange their existing machines. They may design a nice pattern, but they may also have created complex "spaghetti" flow.

- I want you to create a progression of layout designs. First, start with no new machines. Then progressively add new machines in the subsequent designs.

That afternoon the team showed the sensei six different cell designs, complete with data for area and travel distance. Layout #5 is the cleanest. It is the best for space utilization and second best for part travel distance. We have also started looking at what our customer does. Sensei said:

- You should be doing a lot of process Kaizen - otherwise, we will be adding more new machines than necessary.

- Try to combine operations or process steps.

- Your designs are still not good.

The 4 p.m. team leaders' meeting brought two additional comments from the sensei:

- Turnaround time should be part of your layout evaluation matrix.

- I don't understand where on the floor you are going to locate this cell.

Shipping and Receiving Cell Team

In many traditional MRO organizations, the shipping and receiving areas are a mess. In the receiving area, there are piles of boxes containing parts that have been sent for repair by customers, returned from being repaired by outside suppliers, or replaced by suppliers. And, in the shipping area there are boxes containing parts that are either repaired and waiting to be returned to customers or waiting to be sent to outside suppliers for repair. Meanwhile, customers are clamoring for when their repaired parts will be returned, and the cells in the repair operation are anxious to have the next jobs to repair as well as any new parts required for these jobs. The goal of the Shipping and Receiving Cell Team, as outlined at the kickoff meeting, is to create a cell design that will flow smoothly and not be a bottleneck.

Sensei observed:

- You need to create a pull system. But that is not possible today, especially with your major customer.
- Your job is to figure out how to create this pull system, how to deliver to the repair cells, and then how to deliver to your customers when they are done.

At the afternoon meeting the team talked about creating special containers and carts for handling the heavy disks that it receives and ships back to its major customer. They had tried using carts, instead of fork lifts, and had damaged parts when pushing the carts into the shipping ("milk-run") truck. The sensei had the following remarks:

- You need to find a cart that works for here, for the milk-run truck, and at your major customer's site.
- Never place received parts on the floor – it creates stagnation, or "sitting around" time.
- You may not be able to use carts for all of the parts.
- At one of your sister repair operations, they use a conveyor belt to off-load onto a cart. (The belt should not be longer than 5 meters).

The sensei then related a story about soccer:

> I used to coach a kids soccer team. I was informed that the Prince wanted to come and watch a game. The royal office sent three things: a chair, an air conditioner, and a small tent – a fancy enclosure that had the royal family crest on it. Even in the summer the Prince wears a suit, and he must not perspire. The equipment came with a special manual and instructions. We had to post a guard, so that no one would steal the tent or air conditioner, and 24 hours in advance of the game, we had to test the system by having a fully suited person sit in the chair and measure the surrounding temperature. I was that person and had

to wear a suit for the test. The Japanese royal family is very thorough. The Prince came and watched the entire game without incident. I also had to write the speech that he gave after the game.

What is the moral? Think of a disk as the Prince coming to town:

- A special part needs special treatment.
- Consider a special lane dedicated to only disks.
- I want you to take action this week and do something.

The sensei continued his instructions to the team at the 4 p.m. team leaders' meeting:

- Your cell design can have multiple lanes – the number will be determined by the Takt time for each part.
- Your goal this week is to physically create a new lane for disks.
- When you bring parts from your customer, you can use plastic containers. If parts are dirty, take them straight to the clean line and clean them right away.

In response, the general manager remarked that they have carts for 50 percent of the parts, but not for the large drums that need disk replacements.

The next morning, when the team met with the sensei, one of the team members was particularly testy. He wanted to know the difference between a push and a pull system. He noted that at the last Kaizen he had worked on a push system and found that it was not good to hold parts in the receiving well, yet this was the current advice of the sensei. He said that as the customer tears down an engine, the computer system generates a tag for each part. As the repair shop finishes a part, it will induct another part. They receive 40 drums a month and have a capacity to handle two drums per day. When capacity is exceeded, are they to hold the parts and be responsible for the holding time? The sensei responded:

- You must hold the parts in a supermarket.
- Why did the prior supermarket pull system fail? Inspection didn't understand the concept.
- You need to designate a lane for your major customer's parts instead of trying to mix them in with parts from other customers.
- How the parts are pulled is the business of the repair cells, not Shipping and Receiving.
- You should have one lane per cell plus special lanes for your major customer's parts. Don't mix these parts with those from other customers.
- Your supermarket should be visible to the repair cells. It holds parts ahead of the basic inspection operation, that is, ahead of the induction cell.
- What you next need to do is to put tape on the floor to mark out the lanes and see how much space is required.
- The most important thing is for the team to seize the initiative and take ownership. Please do that.

At the 4 p.m. team leaders' meeting, the sensei asked whether the team had decided how many lanes they were going to have and what parts would be assigned to each lane. He was disappointed to hear that the team had focused on just disk replacement for the major customer. He replied:

- You still need to design the lane layout concept and define the maximum number of parts per lane.
- Please do this right away.

End-of-Day Wrap-Ups
The sensei underscored three points in his concluding remarks for the first day:

- Try not to inspect at the end; bring inspection upstream to where the work is being done.
- Injuries happen when operators don't have standard work.
- Remember the order of priority in a Kaizen: safety, quality, productivity.

The sensei spent time scolding the teams at the end of the second day. He told them:

- We have been at this for two days now.

- I know that some of the teams haven't found root causes.

- I know that some teams still don't know what to do. I can see it in the members' eyes: some are shiny and some are not.

- Two teams are shiny and bright. One team had a hard discussion. Those teams that are behind must work harder to catch up.

- Tomorrow, I want the cells on the floor to start taking action. You might fail, but don't worry. Don't spend too much time thinking – just take action.

- Let's not spend the entire week doing simulation. Instead, produce working prototypes that we can use on the floor.

- When you face an obstacle, bring it into the open so that we can take action on it. Talk to your manager and sponsor.

- Your VP comes here every day, because he is interested and willing to support you. The parts for your major customer bother him, and his leader is putting a lot of pressure on him for this operation to improve.

- If you are doing too much, I will stop you. But no one needs to be stopped. That means you need to do more.

Behind the Scenes with Sensei

While walking between the team's locations, the sensei would stop to examine progress charts that had been posted on the walls or on movable boards. One chart in particular that caught his eye was the so-called linearity chart, which plotted actual daily production against a desired linear output that ramped up until it reached the total production goal at the end of the month. He noted to the KPO leader that the data were after the fact, and that there appeared to be a one-week lag between when the production took place and when the chart data were recorded. He admonished that operations must resolve production shortfalls as they occur.

It is noteworthy that our sensei in the previous case study at the hospital talked about the non-linear production that used to exist at an automaker. During that time, he reminisced, operations would wait, idle, for supplier deliveries for the first two weeks of the month and then have to work feverishly during the last part of the month to produce monthly quotas. This is called "dekansho" production, which referred to students who took control of the Japanese university system at the beginning of the 20th Century and would relax, think and sleep for six months and then spend the next six months studying those subjects that appealed to them. One popular subject at the time was philosophy, from which the Japanese word dekansho, which means potato, took on the new, pejorative meaning of lazy or indolent. In this context, the word dekansho was constructed from the first letters of the names of three famous western philosophers, Descartes, Kant and Shopenhauer.

Another recommendation that our sensei had for the KPO leader was to try to find ways to eliminate the requirement for safety glasses in areas that will be visited by customers.

In the break room, a not-so-hidden agenda of the sensei's was playing out. In the shipping and receiving area was an office that was occupying valuable floor space that would be needed for designated receiving lanes in the new cell design. For each of the past five years the sensei had asked the organization to demolish the office. This was the year he resolved to make the tear-down happen, and on Monday he had cleared the idea with senior management and with the Shipping and Receiving Cell Team. In fact, the general manager took responsibility for the work and the VP stood behind his efforts to expedite the necessary paperwork and approvals. The sensei used this example to explain some key points about Kaizen:

- What I have learned about Kaizen is that you must change or even destroy what you have now before you can innovate something new.
- The change could be a physical change or a change in the way you think.
- If you can't do this, then you are not ready for Kaizen.

- There is a famous story about one of our senior sensei who was struggling with an organization to take down a wall to open up more space. Frustrated, the sensei jumped into a forklift and crashed it into the wall. He took this action not to destroy the wall himself but to change the way that people think about what is possible.
- Teams that spend too much time planning or seeking the perfect idea are only pretending to do Kaizen.
- Trust me, my suggestions for action won't negatively impact the business.

The sensei next talked to the KPO leader about the inspection function, which is critical to a repair operation:

- Inspectors must be multi-skilled.
- You need an aisle for inspecting all incoming material. Now, inspection is compartmentalized.
- Other companies have centralized their inspection areas. Everything goes there before being distributed to the other operations. This is inefficient.

Finally, the sensei commented on the culture of the present organization, where relationships and communications between management and associates had been notoriously poor but were now showing signs of improvement. He observed:

- There has been a failure of communications between GM and its people. Now they need a new attitude – they must work together to survive.
- A repair business can bring in a lot of money, but there are also many small companies in competition. They may be invisible to you, but they exist.
- You have an advantage of belonging to a large parent organization that can use its power to attract customers.
- But if you do only the same things that small companies can do, you have no advantage. You must think about how to attract new business.

- It is important for you to improve the communications between management and team members. You must demonstrate a changed leadership attitude.
- It is also important to take one step at a time.

Later, in the quiet room, the sensei offered his wisdom about teams and learning: "My role is to try to find the potential and make it real." Sensei said:

> The Shingijutsu rule is don't teach, at least in a conventional way. I try to help teams discover on their own, and I give teams time to think. Sometimes this leads to the criticism that I am not being prescriptive enough. As a counter example, I would normally have left the drawing of shipping and receiving lanes to the team, but they were not stepping up to this task. I intervened and offered them a solution, because I needed to get one of their influential team members, who had become a vocal critic, on my side. There are times when you must ditch bad teams. You tell the team leader or the uncooperative member to go home and think about the consequences of his actions or inactions, or you may disband the team all together. The sensei who trained me would give a few words of instruction to a team and then let the team figure it out. He would see the solution in his head and then use his vision to guide the team.

NOTES

What did you learn from this chapter?

What will you put into practice?

CHAPTER 7

OFFICE FURNITURE MANUFACTURING KAIZEN

The company in this case study had been working with Shingijutsu since the early 1990s. It manufactures office furniture at multiple locations in the US and would be classified as a high-volume producer that consumes a large amount of supplied materials, including rolled sheet steel, medium-density fiber board, laminates, fabricated components, upholstery fabrics, paint, fasteners and cardboard packing material. The plant we visited has operations related to three types of products: sheet metal (file cabinets, book cases, desks, drawers), wood (desks, bookcases, drawers), and upholstery (desk chairs). The sensei was another of Shingijutsu's senior sensei who was known for getting results with "human-style" genba Kaizen.

Overview

Working in advance with the sensei, the KPO identified six Kaizen teams: Mixed Model Line for File Cabinets, Material Supply for the Mixed Model Line, Die Changeover Reduction, Storage Cabinet Line, Pillow-top Desk Chair Cell, and Cross-cut Saw Cell. The sensei tried to visit each team twice during the day before the 4 p.m. team leaders' meeting. Rather than respond to each team individually after its presentation at the close-out meeting on Friday, the sensei took notes and made one set of concluding remarks to cover everyone. We were not present for the kickoff meeting, so we will start the case study with the individual team perspectives, recount the sensei's remarks at the Wednesday afternoon leaders meeting and at Friday's close-out meeting, and then describe our side meetings with the sensei.

Mixed Model Line Team

The objective of this team was to create a mixed model line for manufacturing two file cabinet models from the current state of one line for each model. In preparation for the Kaizen, and to add a sense of urgency, one of the lines had already been torn down. By the time we caught up with the sensei, this team had been working for two-and-a-half days and had not seemed to understand all that needed to be done. The sensei, desiring to see some progress, made a sketch for them on a flip chart of mixed-model lines. Then he told the team:

- Practice this over and over, and learn something each time.
- The more trials that you make, the more you will realize that you need to understand the operation better.

At the 4 p.m. team leaders' meeting, the team estimated that it could reduce the cycle time by 30 percent. The leader told of the team's plan to run a full mixed-model simulation tomorrow with a radio to signal readiness to induct another job instead of having to walk a joker card from the takeoff point to the induction point. The sensei replied:

- Please do and redo your practice.
- Focus on material flow and on the kind of pull system you need.
- What you are doing is still tantamount to pushing because of your production plan.
- You must accommodate volume fluctuations. Make sure that your pull system can handle them.
- Your first-step basics are to make sure that the line can run both models.
- We can talk about theory, but your success is really about the people. Some people on the line have never built the B product before.
- Managers and supervisors must be working with people on the floor and teaching them the rules of SIQMI (systematic integration of quality, material and information, a system of standard work).

The next morning the team leader told the sensei that he was having difficulty getting the operators to accept the new way of working. The sensei could see that the operators were having difficulty assembling on the moving line and that access to the interior of the file cabinets was difficult because the cabinets were hanging from an overhead trolley at the wrong height. The sensei counseled:

- What you are experiencing is the "unpredictability" of the genba. Use you Kaizen skills to resolve these problems.
- The mixed-model line will save space and energy, but it is not as efficient as dedicated lines.

- You have only one supermarket for this line, so you should move it closer to the line. You must do hand delivery to find problems.

Later during the genba demonstration that replaced the team leaders meeting on the fourth day, he told the team:

- You absolutely need a buffer in your line.
- Keep reworking the line operation.
- Improve cross-training.
- Determine the rate per hour of each model that you must make.
- Define exactly where the supermarket pull signal is.

Material Flow Team for Mixed Model Line

This team was tasked with developing a proper supermarket with delivery runs to supply material to the mixed-model production line for file cabinets. At his morning visit with the team on Wednesday, the sensei asked the team to identify the three principles for the design and operation of a supermarket. The team answered that there must be fixed and labeled addresses for where parts reside, a maximum quantity that may be stored at each address, and a first-in, first-out (FIFO) replenishment system. The sensei seemed pleased and continued:

- You need to establish a rule for how much can be stored at each location in the material supply racks. No rule means no Kaizen.
- Modify your kit carts for material transport to the line as you gain experience. There is no "best." Just keep trying.

During the second visit of the day, the team described its plans to use a small tugger to pull a string of four carts to the production line every hour. Tomorrow the team would start with human-powered carts in an hourly simulation. The team also shared the data that it had gathered about quantities, times and distances. The sensei responded:

- You are in the midst of dramatic changes. It is very important to have a sound design for the supermarket of purchased parts used in the mixed-model production line.

- Think about when you deliver parts to this line. There are two key points for the water striders – a starting time (where on the clock) and a delivery sequence (what is delivered to where).

- Your supermarket store is starting to take shape and will be critical to the line. I use a beer distributor analogy to underscore the importance of supermarket systems: Asahi beer must not be stored to realize its best taste. On the other hand, Budweiser beer is supposed to be stored to achieve its best taste.

The next morning the sensei checked in to witness the team's preparation for its simulation. He asked the team to identify the two keys to Type III standard work, and they wrote down "precise start and end times," followed by a "precise sequence of activities." Again he was pleased. But after rummaging through some of the boxes of parts in the supermarket, he told the team:

- The quantity of parts in your boxes is unknown. You can't do FIFO unless this is known (and visible).

- Also, look to your sister facility for knowledge of how to do small, automatically-guided vehicles.

In the afternoon, the sensei walked along on one of the delivery run simulations. The team reported that it had made several hourly runs that day and had supplied six workstations on each trip. Water striders made the delivery runs using carts; the team had eliminated the use of forklifts. The team also stated that it had consolidated parts for the A model and was starting to consolidate parts for the B model. At the production line, it was obvious that the production material bins were not easily accessible to the water striders; but rearrangement of the production line would be for another day.

Storage Cabinet Line Team
Storage cabinets refer to large, lateral files that are constructed from sheet metal. The production line cell has machines for cutting out

shapes from sheet metal blanks, bending and welding and it has an assembly area. The Amada cutting machine is used for all cabinet models. The team's goals were to increase throughput and decrease turnaround time. When we first intersected the team, the team members were laying out pieces of cardboard and plywood in an outside parking lot in an attempt to improve the cell's layout. The sensei instructed:

- Please walk actual parts through your simulation.
- Include all parts from lines that share the Amada cutting machine.
- Your fishbone has tangled bones.
- You need to change your layout to bring things closer together.
- There is no perfect or wrong layout. There's nothing to worry about.
- Just try different layouts and discover how to improve the layout to make it better.

The next visit to the team was at the genba. Team members had transferred their cardboard cutouts from the parking lot to the floor of the cell, and they had created a scaled, three-dimensional version of the cell using cardboard cutouts on a table-top. The team had gathered data from production runs made with 10 operators in the cell. He said:

- Please look at how material flow works in the various layouts.
- With reduced volumes, you have demonstrated that you can operate with fewer people.
- You need to have enough machine capacity at bottlenecks.
- The operators must not interfere with one another; the standard work combination sheet will help show this.
- I think that your target may be too easy. Please take the challenge to operate with fewer than 10 people.

In the morning the sensei returned to the genba. The sensei looked at the yamazumi chart and showed the team that Takt time was in range. He did not like the layout - there was still too much travel, so he engaged with the team in rearranging the cell with the aid of the table-top model. He instructed the team:

- Show pictures of all parts in the table-top layout.
- See how the parts flow. Then slide everything closer together.
- Create standard work combination sheets to validate the layout – the operators' motions and the configuration.
- Show operators in the layout.
- Record the cycle times for each work station and include machine cycle times.
- Can you devise a simple, one-number code for changing over the cutting program for the Amada cutting machine?

That afternoon at the genba simulation, the sensei had more advice:

- Move the Amada and Ras machines closer to the point of use.
- Assign the Ras operator, as he gets ahead, to help with the Amada machine.
- It is important to continue to work on the layout.
- Focus first on material flow, then look at the operators.
- Define which processes each operator is responsible for, then these assignments will become part of the yamazumi charts.
- When will you move the equipment to rearrange the cell? Tonight? Tomorrow?

Pillow-Top Desk Chair Line Team

Like the other production cell teams, this team had the goal of improving its operation. In the first part of the week, the team had made progress in balancing the individual process steps and reducing the distance traveled by operators. The sensei asked the team to create bar charts of the cycle time for each operation. He told the team:

- You will see the cycle times continue to change as you distribute and balance work.

- If the cycle times are less than the Takt time, your cell design should work.
- But volumes will continue to change. Your cell has to be flexible enough to handle both increased and decreased volume.

Figure 7-1 Team members practicing material hand-off.

The next afternoon during the genba tour, the team reported that it had eliminated two operators by balancing workloads. Now each operator did approximately four tasks. The sensei said:

- Make sure that you have standard work for six, seven or eight people in the cell to handle volume reductions and increases.
- Your operators will need to be cross-trained for these configurations.

Blanking Line Setup Reduction Team
The blanking machine is a large punch press that die cuts a continuous roll of sheet metal into two-dimensional patterns or blanks for

downstream operations. The goal of this team was to speed up the die changeover process. At the afternoon leaders meeting, the team leader reported that the team had missed its changeover target today. But it did improve standard work and made two safety improvements (implementing lockout-tagout for the machine and bolting down the die rack) and two quality improvements, one related to increasing the lighting levels at the inspection table. The team had also started to record the amount of scrap produced following a setup. For tomorrow the team planned to capture as many setups as possible and to update and post the quality standards. The sensei noted:

- Standard work for setup is critical.
- Any changeover is an opportunity for Kaizen.
- Your task is to perform the external setup operations stably and consistently.
- I look forward to seeing your results tomorrow.

At the next morning meeting with the sensei, the team showed data for their last setup; the time had come down considerably. After walking upstream to inspect the rolls of sheet steel that were waiting to be mounted on the line, the sensei observed:

- You need to eliminate the handling damage on the steel rolls.
- Also, do something about the trash in the area. This is part of Kaizen.

Later in the day the team leader revealed that the team's data for setup time were not uniform. The sensei remarked:

- A key thing is to conduct the external setup tasks correctly.
- It will be difficult for this to take root. Spend time to develop the habit.
- Look at internal setup tasks and standard work.
- Make sure that the next coil is properly loaded.
- Practice, practice, practice.

Cross-Cut Saw Line Team

This team was setting up a new cell built around a cross-cut saw on a gantry to cut medium-density fiberboard panels to the sizes needed for simulated-wood office furniture products. The team was following the Production Preparation Process (3P). The sensei related to us that by the end of the first day, the team had completed laying out, on the floor of an empty building, two-dimensional cardboard cutouts of the equipment in the cell. The team thought that it was done; whereupon the sensei informed the members that they had not even started, and that he wanted them to make a three-dimensional mockup of the cell and everything that goes with it. The sensei's mantra for the week became "3P means 3D."

By the time of our visit on the afternoon of the third day, the team had created out of cardboard a full-scale model of the saw table and gantry. There was also a scissor table on wheels for removing the cut blanks from the saw table and rolling them to raised roller conveyors (simulated by wooden platforms) on the floor. Each different kind of blank had its own conveyor from which the cut blanks would be removed and transported by forklift to the appropriate furniture line. The sensei said:

- In your simulation, show me one pattern being cut.
- Try to eliminate the forklift. Use a trolley or a tugger.
- You need to maximize material utilization.
- If I say too much to you, you will only follow what I say and this will limit your thinking.

Next morning the team had manufactured wooden carts on wheels for transporting the cut blanks from the roller conveyors. The sensei noted that the team would need 200 of these carts to handle a day's output of cut blanks, and that this seemed like an expensive solution.

The simulation that afternoon was quite convincing, and the sensei was pleased to see that the managers and supervisors participated and got their hands dirty. He remarked:

- Why are there five lanes? Can you make do with three lanes, or even one? Try to save space.

- Think about locating the saw in an empty place in the plant.
- You have shown us how to bring three dimensions to cardboard cutouts. This will be a new rule for 3P.

Wrap-Up to Team Leaders Meeting

The sensei took notes during the team leaders' presentations and then gave the following summary:

- I can see dramatic changes taking place, although I know that some teams are struggling.
- I looked at the paint line and was surprised to see colors like "Carnival" Orange and "Parakeet" Green coming off the line. But this is a good sign, because it means that you are trying to satisfy your customers.
- There is a common theme to these teams – you are trying to run families of similar models on the same production line.
- Remember the three conditions for a supermarket – fixed address, maximum quantity, and FIFO (arranged so that the water strider can pick up material easily)
- For everyone, including the management, it is important to pick up any trash that you see on the floor. You need to get out of the habit of walking by abnormalities without resolving them.
- An impressive example that I saw was the stopping of the paint line because of an abnormality. The people on the line were called together and the abnormality was explained to them.
- Now you need to take the next step and determine root causes.

Close-Out Remarks

Again the sensei took notes and addressed the teams and their sponsors and the senior management after all final presentations were completed:

- I wish to thank all six teams.

- At the Monday kickoff, I promised to visit the genba, and I did so many times. I saw that many got their hands dirty. I also saw lots of trash on the floor and people starting to pick it up.

- It is important to keep up your momentum.

- There has been a long history of Kaizen at this company. Volumes have tended to go up, and I think that we have gotten used to this trend and are getting stale.

- The Kaizen projects this week selected goals and took different vantage points. People were surprised by what could be achieved, especially the saw team. They learned the importance of 3D.

- Two of the teams worked on standard work.

- We must always go back to basics. What are the basics? i) Standard work. Everyone – managers, engineers, operators – must understand standard work. Through standard work, everyone comes together, and ii) Go to the genba, where everything resides, to see waste.

- There are now big fluctuations in volume. This changes everything and really puts pressure on understanding the basics.

- Why is there so much inventory on your lines? You need rules and standard work for water striders – precise start and end times for their delivery runs and a precise delivery sequence. Make sure that the order of material delivery is clear. Repeat material deliveries over and over; collect times and improve the process.

- You should have a big rule for all lines – no pallets on them. Break down pallets outside of the line and deliver only what's needed. For example, what would you do if a big pallet of beer were delivered to your kitchen?

- Work with suppliers to enforce your supermarket rules – fixed addresses, maximum quantities, and FIFO. If you have local suppliers, reduce their quantities.

- We will see many more examples of the need for mixed model lines. The secrets are standard work and cross-training.

- For the set-up reduction team, keep talking among yourselves and learning from practice.

Behind the Scenes with Sensei

After the close-out meeting, we asked the sensei if he has an evaluation scale for teams. He told us that he does not, because it depends on the genba and there are just too many variables.

We asked about how he selected the Kaizen projects for this week. He said that he gave the organization homework during his last visit two-and-a-half years ago, and that he would check periodically (from a distance) about what had been done and whether there were any new strategic priorities or immediate needs. Then he and the KPO director jointly decided what should be done. From this point the sensei explained:

> "At the start of the Kaizen week, some teams didn't want to do very much work. For example, the Storage Cabinet and Cross-cut Saw teams thought that they could just layout some cardboard cutouts on the floor and be finished. I encouraged both teams to go much farther. I told the Crosscut Saw team to go to 3D and actually model the saw, the carts and the material flow. I also encouraged the Storage Cabinet team to focus on material flow in their cell layout."

Sensei then elaborated on the importance of people in Kaizen, and that nobody must be harmed by Kaizen.

> A sensei must understand that Kaizen is about people. If there is not management agreement up-front that the Kaizen will not cost people their jobs, then sensei will not come. Management has the opportunity to reduce people through attrition. That means that if 10 people leave, then management should hire back only two people instead of 10. The productivity gained from Kaizen will make up the difference. You can also use temporary or contract labor and overtime to solve the problem of a small workforce until Kaizen productivity gains are realized.

It is also not uncommon for clients of Shingijutsu to share experiences and to help one another. The presence of "outside eyes" on a Kaizen team can be very beneficial.

During a break on Thursday, we asked sensei to share his vision for Shingijutsu for the next 100 years: What will Shingijutsu look like 100 years from now? He thought that Shingijutsu would continue to evolve. He allowed the possibility that the company might lose its way, but this would be a sign of progress. The sensei suggested looking at the characteristics distinguishing companies that have been in existence for 100 years or more from companies that had gone out of business. He observed that things fell apart for those companies that became too comfortable.

We also asked the sensei to talk about what makes Shingijutsu different. He found this a tough question, because of the company's cultural legacy of humility, but he came up with two reasons. The first was the emphasis on basics, the fundamentals. The second was the emphasis on the genba, where the real work of an organization is done, not in a classroom somewhere. He continued that at the genba we can discuss or debate the nature of reality and we can learn things. He invoked a metaphor that at the genba we can learn to eat; then we can learn to eat more efficiently.

The sensei added a third dimension – attention to people. He said that Shingijutsu focuses on developing people and making them stronger. He asserted that whatever you do, if people do not grow, you have wasted your time. He noted that a sensei must measure how many people are growing; that is, how many people will tackle abnormalities and not want to escape from it?

He also mentioned the role of speed in education – speed forces you to act, and through action you learn. He cited the example of a sailing yacht. When the wind blows hard, the yacht resists turning over. You do not see it, but the mechanism is there.

NOTES

What did you learn from this chapter?

What will you put into practice?

PART IV

EVER LASTING AND
EVER CHANGING

*Too many people think they know
the basics when they do not.*

CHAPTER 8

BASICS

"Back to basics" is a theme that pervades each Shingijutsu engagement, especially those with long-term customers. It expresses the sensei's desire for an organization to reacquaint itself with the foundation of its learning before taking on advanced topics in genba Kaizen. Sometimes, as we saw in the case of the hospital, the sensei will conduct a tutorial on the basic principles. Other times, as we saw in the cases of the original equipment manufacturer and the repair operation, the sensei will weave descriptions of the basic principles into his daily remarks. Recall the situation of the machine uptime team in the case study of the repair operation, where the sensei terminated the team's Kaizen activities and instructed the team to implement the basics of total productive maintenance before doing anything else.

During his work with a team, the sensei will also probe the team's level of understanding of the basics by asking questions – for example, "What are the three properties of a supermarket or the two conditions of Type III standard work?" Or, by singling out a team member to describe what a particular principle means to him or her. One team member, a high-level executive, remembers vividly the time that the sensei asked her on the spot to teach a study-mission class about the "heart of Kaizen." After a few seconds of thought, she spoke about the human dimension – what Kaizen means to people and their motivation and fulfillment.

Just what are the basics? They include behavior and attitudes, system thinking, customer value, standard work (Takt, sequence, SWIP), 5S, flow, pull, genba observation with all senses, root causes analysis, quick action, mistake-proofing, eliminating muda, cost (genka) reduction, supermarkets, heijunka, kanban, jidoka or autonomation, hanedashi or automatic unloading, machine management, just in time, water striders transportation carts, no work/full work, quick and dirty, moonshine, fast changeover, early warning (Andon), making profit, policy deployment, and more.

Behind these concepts of genba Kaizen are numerous tools and methods to understand the current state and create an improved future state followed by more Kaizen. For example, hoshin kanri, 3P, Process-at-a-Glance chart, Material and Information Flow Map, Functional Analysis, Concept Generation from Nature, Concept Selection, Fishbone Chart, 5 Why's Analysis, Spaghetti Diagram, Standard Work Combination Sheet, Yamazumi Chart, Standard Work Sheet, Single Minute Exchange of Die, and Total Productive Maintenance, to name several. There are also evolving checklists for the best practices of world-class manufacturing and logistics operations; not surprisingly, the practices on these checklists fall under the headings of safety, quality and productivity.

The purpose of this chapter is not to replay a description of each of the basics, which have generally been well covered elsewhere. Rather, our intention is to introduce some new concepts and to correct concepts that clients may not have understood well or may have incorrectly implemented. We will start with the human perspective of Kaizen, because it is so often brushed aside by organizations anxious to deploy the tools and methods for improving safety, quality, and productivity.

Heart of Kaizen

In our case studies and in the earlier description of Shingijutsu's values and culture, we have encountered in different guises the philosophy that "Kaizen is about people and growing their capabilities." This idea dovetails with descriptions of the learning process whose purpose is to increase an individual's ability to take effective action. One senior sensei put it this way: "If people don't grow, then we have failed." We have also seen that a skilled sensei has many ways of engaging the hearts of people – their spirits and passions. Sometimes the sensei scolds, sometimes he humiliates, sometimes he appeals to common sense, sometimes he uses humor or play acting, sometimes he tells stories or invokes analogies, sometimes he encourages ("Don't worry, you won't fail. Just try it."), sometimes he demonstrates a teaching principle, and sometimes he pitches in and gets his hands dirty. In all cases the sensei is trying to promote, through reflection and action, the learning and growth of team members at all levels of the organization. He knows that he has succeeded when everyone in the organization has a "good heart," as measured by their passion to make their organization the best in the world.

Figure 8-1 Team member reflecting on his discoveries and learnings.

The practice of basics (kihon) involves three human virtues:

- Honesty
- Humility
- Thoroughness

The first virtue means to tell the truth – to face reality as it is, not as you would like it to be. It is common for a sensei to tell a team, "You lied to me," after discovering that an actual situation was not as portrayed by the team. Often the sensei will embellish his response with an appropriate amount of disgust to underscore the point. Telling lies (koshakushi) is inimical to Kaizen. On the other hand, when a sensei points out to a team that its charts or data are lying, the sensei is usually impugning the team's methods and not its integrity.

The second is humility, which means to set aside your ego so that it won't impair your learning process. One of our sensei noted that teams, after making gains through Kaizen, have a tendency to become "snobby." He admonishes everyone, "However great you may think you are, you are not perfect and still have much to improve; somewhere in the world there is someone who is better than you." A visit to a famous Japanese automaker begins with an apology for the state in which the visitor will find the plant.

In the three case studies, we have seen how the sensei gently bring humility to a team, for example, with the observation, "You are good, but not that good." When the situation warrants, the sensei may scold a person or a team with the statement "You're fired!" The gentler version is "Please go away and think about how your poor attitude is affecting your team."

The third virtue, thoroughness, is called "teti" in Japanese. In the context of kihon it means finding all root causes, exploring all options, and identifying and eliminating all waste. It means looking at things in sufficient detail to understand them. It means turning up the power of one's virtual microscope to see even more details. It means going to the genba to see for yourself. It means validating performance through action, not paper studies. It means considering all dimensions of Kaizen – safety, quality and productivity. It means getting everything done.

SIQMI

SIQMI (pronounced *shi-koo-me*) stands for Systematic Integration of Quality, Material and Information. It refers to an operating system of standard work in Shingijutsu's practice. There is a distinction between a SIQMI and a practice. In the case of the hospital's policy deployment team, for example, the development of a policy is a practice; whereas, the recognition of the need for a policy, the dovetailing of the policy with the organization's strategic plans, the development of the policy, the deployment of the policy to the organization, and the subsequent monitoring of the effectiveness of the policy and identification of the need to make corrections to it requires an operating system or SIQMI. Sensei will often tell a team, you are viewing your task as a practice, but you really need to see your task as developing a SIQMI. In other words, elevate your sphere of thought and action to the system level.

A prevalent failure among teams occurs when a team stops short of investigating system effects in a root causes analysis. This fault can effectively derail a Kaizen, sending it off in the wrong direction or focusing it on fixing a symptom as opposed to developing a permanent, preventative solution. We saw earlier several instances of the lack of system thinking in the case studies of Chapters 5, 6, and 7. For example, the hospital sterilization team concentrated on improving the washing process without asking the system-level questions of why are there so many things to wash, and are there ways to prevent them from getting dirty in the first place?

Similarly, the machine uptime team at the repair operation didn't understand that one of the root causes of the low machine availability was the failure of Manufacturing Technical Services to implement a Total Productive Maintenance system and culture. Another concern was that system-level analyses and business cases were not being done to determine whether it would be better to keep and repair old machines or to purchase new machines.

A final example is the policy deployment team at the hospital. Although this team had gathered data from the staff about the policy deployment process, the root causes of the poor policy compliance were not investigated. The result was that the team started with a clean sheet of paper and had to rediscover some previous lessons about how the hospital's current operating system was defeating policy deployment.

5S

Next on the list of basics requiring new understanding is 5S. As we listened to the Jutsu Shu talk about 5S, we realized with a sinking feeling that the two major international companies for which we had worked had not understood the intent of 5S. New to us was the philosophy that some elements of 5S – the troublesome ones involving sweeping and cleaning or sanitizing – should actually be treated as negative goals; that is, the less, the better. Instead of improving cleanliness, the real intent of this part of 5S is to avoid making a mess that requires cleaning in the first place.

Another misunderstanding, this time with the second S (interpreted as "straighten"), had also been ingrained. Straighten has been interpreted as lining things up in neat rows or stacks, but this arrangement is not helpful, if the material for the next job is buried in a neat pile or in the middle of a straight row that is difficult to access. We concluded that 5S had not been correctly understood and implemented at our companies. In fact, the implementation had alienated people to the point that people resisted 5S.

The KPO director of the hospital in the case study had the same reaction. The sensei apologized and said that Shingijutsu was at fault for not having been clearer in its teaching of 5S. He noted that the translations of 5S to English are shallow and have lost the intent of 5S. To correct this error, we present Shingijutsu's explanation of 5S.

In the beginning, there were only two S's – Seiri (Sort, organize) and Seiton (Straighten, set in order). The idea of Seiri (sort) is to throw out what is not needed, to remove impediments to work. The second S, Seiton, means to order or arrange things so that they are immediately accessible or retrievable. It means to put everything needed for a job within an operator's reach or point of use – in the quantity needed and when the operator needs it. The root "ton" in Seiton has the connotation of immediate, instant, or one touch. Taken together, the first two S's hold the prescription for Just-in-Time. We don't believe that this tight connection between 5S and flow production had been appreciated, as most people view 5S as something extra.

The translation of Seiton as "straighten" fuels misconceptions about the word's true meaning, because in English straighten means to "line up in a straight row or file." Having straight rows or stacks of material doesn't help productivity, if an operator has to search through a row or dig to the bottom of a stack to find the next part to work on. Similarly, arranging a cell in a U-shape, not a straight line, makes the equipment in the cell more accessible to an operator and reduces travel distance.

The third S, Seisou (Sweep, clean), means to sweep away or clean up things such as dirt, dust, chips, germs, spills and trash from the workplace. It refers to the act of cleaning and is often interpreted as "shine" in English. However, the word shine can lead to excess. The fourth S, Seiketsu (Sanitary, clean), has the meaning of sustaining a state of cleanliness or sanitation. Together these two S's have very practical implications for safety, quality and productivity. Dirt, dust, chips, germs, spills and trash present slip and biological hazards, and they also represent foreign objects that can intrude on the performance of processes or that can infiltrate products and compromise their reliability.

The level of cleanliness, sanitation or sterility required depends on the process and the application. For example, microelectronics fabrication must be carried out in Class A clean rooms; the operating room in a hospital and the surgical implements used must be sterile; there must be no foreign objects present in an aircraft gas-turbine engine test cell; and there must be no sources of electrostatic discharge in the assembly area for electronic instruments and computers. Then there is the psychological impact of a clean workplace on human productivity: a dingy workplace fails to inspire motivation. On the other hand, forcing people to maintain an overly organized and clean workplace is also not healthy for morale.

Now comes the surprise. The implication of Seisou and Seiketsu is not to do more cleaning and shining (painting) but to find ways to reduce the amount of time spent on sweeping or cleaning and on keeping the workplace sanitary or sterile. The objective is how to avoid making a mess once the workplace is at the appropriate level of cleanliness. This objective is an example of SIQMI (system) thinking and it brings into focus the role of the fifth S, Shitsuke (discipline).

Through constant management attention and peer pressure, the organization needs to enforce the discipline associated with the first four S's.

An essential part of the discipline of 5S is being able to detect or sense abnormalities in a process, so that fast action can be taken to restore the process to normality. We have seen how, through the practice of standing in the "observation circle" at the genba, sensei train team members to sharpen their skills of observation and to engage all of their senses. Augmenting human capabilities for sensing are visual controls and technology for machine condition monitoring. Visual controls tell the observer at a glance what the current state of production is, and whether it is on track to meet the day's customer demand. Andon lights, whether human or machine operated, signal normal operation (green), slowed operation (yellow), or stopped operation (red). Teams are also encouraged to incorporate sensors in their machines that will automatically shut down a machine as soon as a defect occurs. This practice is called jidoka.

We will end this piece with a personal anecdote, in which we recall reading the report from a group of executives who had returned from a study mission in Japan. An overriding observation was: "Our factories have better 5S than their factories do." We now understand that the executives were comparing shininess of the factories and had clearly missed the deeper meanings of 5S.

Vision

One client confided in the sensei, "We have either lost our vision or not gotten a vision of our future state. We seem to be overly focused on our current state, as you can see from our charts on the wall." The sensei reacted with following wisdom:

- You need to have five views – see the mountain (the business), see the forest (factory), see the tree (individual production line), see the branch (operator), and see the leaf (individual movement or action).
- The tree is where you are, the forest is what you see nearby, and the mountain is the distant, birds-eye view.
- These define where you are standing now, where you want to go, and the direction in which you are currently heading.
- Translated into time, the three views are: today, tomorrow and the distant future.
- In your particular case, you need to understand your process capability. Sun Tzu once said that, if you know your enemy's capacity and your own capacity is greater than his, then you can start a war and win.
- Subsequently you can think about how to become flexible in responding to increases and decreases in demand, which seems to be your vision. For example, you have to pay for space even when you don't use it. Can you make some areas like a tent that you fold up when not in use?
- Another part of flexibility is being able to do things in a short time. My rule is that you should be able to respond in about 16 seconds, the time to take one breath and hold it comfortably.

- Your planning is based on forecasting. If you are able to respond quickly to a situation, you can reduce your planning horizon. Think about how to win at roulette – the later you can delay the croupier from closing off bets, the slower the wheel will be rotating, and the more likely it is that you can tell in which slot the ball will drop.

- Two kinds of people can help you with visioning. The first kind are called bakshin; they tell you things you don't know in a very harsh manner. The second kind are called shinka; they are colleagues who follow you around and tell you the truth. You also need a master. These positions come from the days of dynasties but they are still very useful in today's world.

Process Mapping

The roles of various process mapping methods do not seem to be well understood by many of Shingijutsu's clients. We see confusion over the appropriate uses of Material and Information Flow Diagrams (popularly known as Value Stream Maps), Process Flow Analysis, and Process-at-a-Glance charts. We think that the following clarifications are in order.

The Material and Information Flow Diagrams are best suited for identifying waste (muda) at a high level, where the process elements appear to be transactional. If it contains more than eight to ten major process elements, then the level of detail will start to confound the "big" picture. The primary data are time-based: Takt time, lead times, cycle times, process times, changeover times, and machine availability times. Time is a major marker of waste: if the cycle time of a process step is longer than the Takt time, or if the process time is much less than the cycle time, or if changeover times are long, or if machine availability time is low, or if order fulfillment (lead) times are long, there is waste. The data also show inventory or job queues, first pass yields, and the number of people required to perform each process element.

Information technology applications in use at each process element are also indicated. A separate box representing the customer shows customer order data, including model volume for a period, pack quantities, and shipment frequency. The diagram starts with an order or requirement from the customer and ends with a delivery of the order or required work product or service back to the customer. Information generally flows from right to left across the top half of the diagram, and material generally flows from left to right across the bottom half of the diagram.

The Material and Information Flow Diagram does not show the functional organizations that support the process elements. Instead, it is focused on getting the work accomplished. The representation is not particularly well suited to diagramming rework loops (recall its transactional basis), but the existence of rework can be seen in first-pass yield numbers and in differences between cycle and process times. The representation does support forward branching, for example, decisions to process a job in-house vs. outsourcing the job.

The Material and Information Flow Diagram has two versions: one for the current state; the other for the future state. The current state is based on the most recent data that the Kaizen team has been able to record at the genba by walking the process in the direction of its finish to its start. After completing the current state diagram, the Kaizen team identifies the major wastes and impediments that it deems important to eliminate, each waste elimination task becoming the subject of another Kaizen.

On the assumption that all of these Kaizens will be successful, the team redraws the diagram to create the future state diagram. In this respect, the future state diagram is often called "paper" Kaizen – it is a wish until the activities are actually completed and the outcomes are confirmed.

The Material and Information Flow Diagram is very useful for prioritizing which major process elements need attention. For example, in the case study of the hospital sterilization process, the washing element stood out as a bottleneck (but certainly not the only source of waste in the round trip that surgical implements made from the operating room). Once a major process element is highlighted for further investigation, then the Kaizen team needs to understand the details of the underlying sub-process steps, tasks and activities.

Two additional process techniques are useful for capturing the next level of detail. One is Process Flow Analysis chart and the other is the Process-at-a-Glance chart. The Process Flow Analysis chart represents how the work in a process is deployed to the various functional entities in the organization, and it shows how the functional entities interact and make decisions during the flow of work through the organization. Work is generally represented at the task level, in which a task may contain several activities that are not shown.

Time runs notionally from left to right, although the Process Flow Analysis chart also shows rework loops and loop backs when the conditions for a decision are not met. It is important to record how many times work cycles through a loop before exiting. Date for segment times can also be shown across the bottom. The Process Flow Analysis chart reveals the effects of inadequate communication, mistakes in work instructions, dropped or late handoffs between functions, inferior design of work products, and poor quality of execution. It is a fruitful place to start a root causes investigation to explain the system-level abnormalities seen in the Material and Information Flow Diagrams for the current state.

Shingijutsu's production method can be described as harmony between people, material, information and machines. The Jutsu Shu often cites the analogy of a piano player. To produce the music intended by its composer, the piano must be in tune and the musician must be skilled in reproducing the foot, hand and finger movements inferred by the notes and tempos shown in the musical score. The appropriate tool for breaking a process down into this level of detail is the Process-at-a-Glance chart.

As recounted in the case study of the hospital sterilization team, the sensei requested the team to add the following details to the chart: purpose, need and current state data for quantity, quality and timing, including WIP and frequency. Under tools he also asked the team to identify those tools (dogu) that are unique to the hospital (i.e., specially designed for the hospital's sterilization process) vs. those tools (kogo) that are commercially available.

Functional Analysis

Another weakness we frequently see in teams is their inability to perform sound functional analysis. Being able to breakdown a product or a process into the functions it performs is absolutely essential to Kaizen, because this discipline is the foundation for the creative generation of improvement concepts. Once a key function is identified, the Kaizen team can look to nature, science and technology, and other sources for different ways in which this function is performed. Putting together a similar list of options for each of the functions involved in a product or process generates a large number of new improvement concepts, from which Shingijutsu advises the team to pick seven for further study.

Fine Points

- Just as there is no "m" in kanban, there is no "m" in genba.
- Muda (waste) is a compound of two words: mu (no) and da (money). It means waste, anything that doesn't make money for either the customer or our company.
- Don't refer to a Material and Information Flow Diagram as a Value Stream Map. It shows waste, not value.
- 3P means 3D. Use three-dimensional models in the Production Preparation Process.

Key Findings

We end this chapter with a summary of the key findings that define Shingijutsu's philosophy:

- Kaizen is about people. Improvement must not result in layoffs.
- Safety first. Then quality and productivity.
- Get the facts at the genba and don't take shortcuts.
- Don't teach. Help people discover knowledge on their own. Turn questions into self-study assignments.
- Promote a bias for action and practice. They are essential to learning.
- Correction, even scolding, improves the performance of both individuals and teams.

- Details are necessary, but don't get lost in them. Always keep the big picture in view.
- Fit the application to the principle, not the other way around. Don't bend time-tested principles.
- Modify the business to conform to Kaizen, not the reverse.
- Be humble, self-effacing, and thorough.

In summary, successful Kaizen requires understanding the basics (kihon).

NOTES

What did you learn from this chapter?

What will you put into practice?

CHAPTER 9

THE FUTURE

This book had shared with you our understanding of the spirit, mindset, and methods of Shingijutsu USA Corporation consultants and their approach to improving the human condition. As we said at the start, it is derived from our participation in Kaizen, our observation of Kaizen, and our study of Kaizen. Shingijutsu's practice of Kaizen evolves over time in response to changing conditions. This will continue to be the case far into the future, where the challenges facing business and society are sure to be great.

Shingijutsu and those trained in genba Kaizen must step forward and create a future where humans can thrive. Together we must change ways of thinking through practice and reflection, and guide people in eliminating waste from all sources through genba Kaizen.

Shingijutsu's approach has been to eliminate waste a few industrial clients at a time and, generally, from the viewpoint of production. There are significant opportunities in the infrastructure arena, where overruns of schedules and costs are rampant, and where there are structural abnormalities associated with new work.

There could be immense benefit from the 3P (Production Preparation Process) methodology to eliminate waste in pre-production processes. There is a large opportunity to integrate Kaizen in strategic planning processes in companies large and small, in government, and in non-governmental organizations, to eliminate Muda.

There is important work ahead to create a better future for both people and the natural world. This will be indispensable for achieving harmony between people and Planet. We must begin at the genba, master the basics, and do so on a scale larger than has ever been done before.

ABOUT THE AUTHORS

Ralph Wood

Dr. Wood spent his career in industrial research and development as practicing engineer, program team leader, manager, and consultant. He started with GEs Knolls Atomic Power Laboratory as a lead engineer in the methods development group for the thermo-hydraulic design of naval reactors. Subsequent to that, he worked at GEs Corporate Research & Development Center and was a principal author of GEs winning proposal for DARPAs Initiative in Concurrent Engineering.

At United Technologies Corporation, he managed the Product Development and Manufacturing Department at the Research Center, subsequently heading the Management of Technology Department. He later became director of UTCs quality and productivity operating system, Achieving Competitive Excellence (ACE).

Dr. Wood was responsible for overhauling UTCs "Passport" stage-gated product development process, for leading the incorporation of Lean thinking into ACE, and for supporting the redesign of the Research Center's innovation process. He was also a member of the team that founded a major corporate initiative called Operation Transformation that involved UTCs supply base in cost reduction via quality and productivity improvement, and a main designer of UTCs current Quality University.

After retiring from UTC Ralph founded a consulting and teaching company, Accelerating Excellence LLC, dedicated to improving the quality and productivity of enterprises.

Dr. Wood is chairman emeritus of the Connecticut Audubon Society. As a member of the Mentoring Corps for Community Development, he teaches STEM topics to middle school students in two school districts.

Dr. Wood holds Sc.B., Sc.M., and Ph.D. degrees in mechanical engineering from Brown University.

Michael Herscher

Michael Herscher worked for The Boeing Company for nearly 30 years and held a variety of positions including: Tool and Production Planner, Personnel Supervisor, Compensation Manager, and Corporate Labor Relations Manager. Subsequently he became Director Continuous Quality Improvement (fabrication division), and Director of Manufacturing Support Services.

Michael's education in Kaizen with Chihiro Nakao began while he was Director of Tier Three Parts Provisioning. Subsequent to that, he was promoted to Director Lean Enterprise Office (Kaizen Promotion Office) Boeing Commercial Airplanes Group. He retired from Boeing in 2008.

Michael's attended Washington State University on an athletic scholarship (gymnastics), but left after one year to volunteer to work with Cesar Chavez and the United Farm Workers. He spent a little over two years with Chavez, with his last assignment as a security guard. Michael returned home to Kent Washington and went to work for a network of food banks, Neighbors In Need, now Northwest Harvest, as a warehouse supervisor. He left Neighbors In Need to run his own businesses, a stuffed toy business, two arcades, and a retail furniture business.

Subsequent to that, he went to work for Boeing Commercial Airplanes and returned to college nights and weekends. He graduated from City University of Seattle with a degree in Business Administration.

Herscher has been married for over 40 years and has two adult children. He is a Shodan (1st degree black belt) Shotokan Karate of America.

Bob Emiliani

Dr. Emiliani is a former manager at Pratt & Whitney, a unit of United Technologies Corporation, where he was trained in genba Kaizen by Shingijutsu. He had responsibility for implementing flow production in the manufacturing shop floor as a business unit manager and supply networks as a purchasing and supply chain manager.

After working in industry for 12 years, Bob joined academia. He was the first academic to focus on Lean leadership as an area of scholarly research and is a leading figure dedicated to helping people correctly understand and practice Lean management. He is recognized for his decades of work to advance the "Respect for People" principle, as well as the development of innovative new methods for improving leadership.

Dr. Emiliani is currently a professor at a university in Connecticut and has pioneered the application of Lean principles and practices in academic processes in higher education. He is the author of 15 books on various aspects of Lean leadership and Lean management.

Dr. Emiliani holds a Ph.D. in Materials Engineering from Brown University; an M.S. degree in Chemical Engineering from the University of Rhode Island; and a B.S. degree in Mechanical Engineering from the University of Miami.

Emiliani has been married for 30 years and has two adult children.

For more information, please visit www.bobemiliani.com www.leanprofessor.com.

Printed in Great Britain
by Amazon

78694651R00078